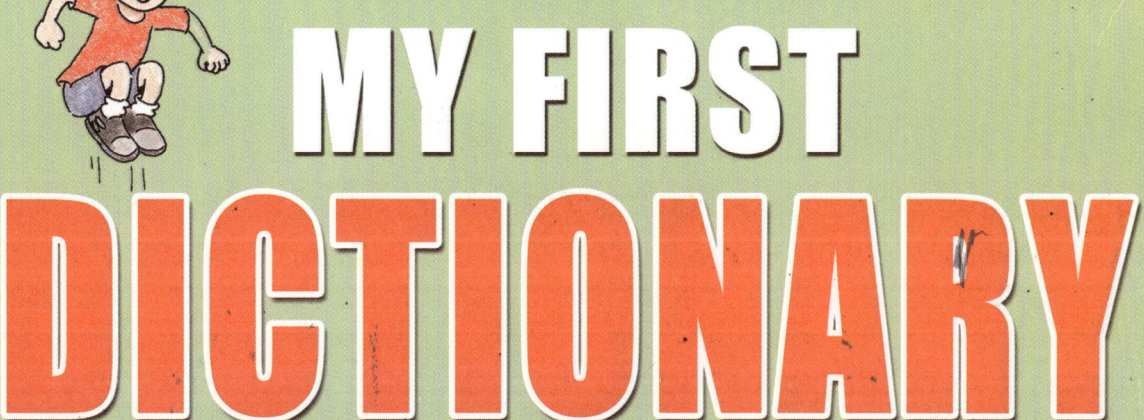

MY FIRST DICTIONARY

STERLING

Using Your Dictionary

Before we learn how to use a dictionary, let us first learn the meaning of the word "dictionary". A dictionary is a book which tells us the meaning of words, how to pronounce them, how to spell them and how the words are used. Using a dictionary helps us to speak and write correctly, expand our vocabulary and it serves as a wonderful guidebook to the English language for every young reader.

About My First Dictionary

- Each headword has been carefully selected to help build the vocabulary for every young reader.
- The words are listed alphabetically from A to Z making it simple for the child to find the words.
- Guide words tell you the first and last headwords that appear on each page.
- The meaning of each word has been written in simple language so that the child will be able to understand the meanings easily. The definitions speak to the child directly enabling the child to read and understand the words and meanings easily and independently.
- Colourful pictures are used to make the meanings of each word even easier to understand.
- Each headword includes a simple pronunciation guide which spells the words the way they sound and how they should be pronounced.
- Some of the words also have n. or v. after the pronunciation These show whether a word is a noun or a verb. A noun (n.) is a word we use for a person, place, animal or thing. A verb (v.) shows us that the word describes an action.
- What you will also find is a reference guide to send the reader to other parts of the dictionary.

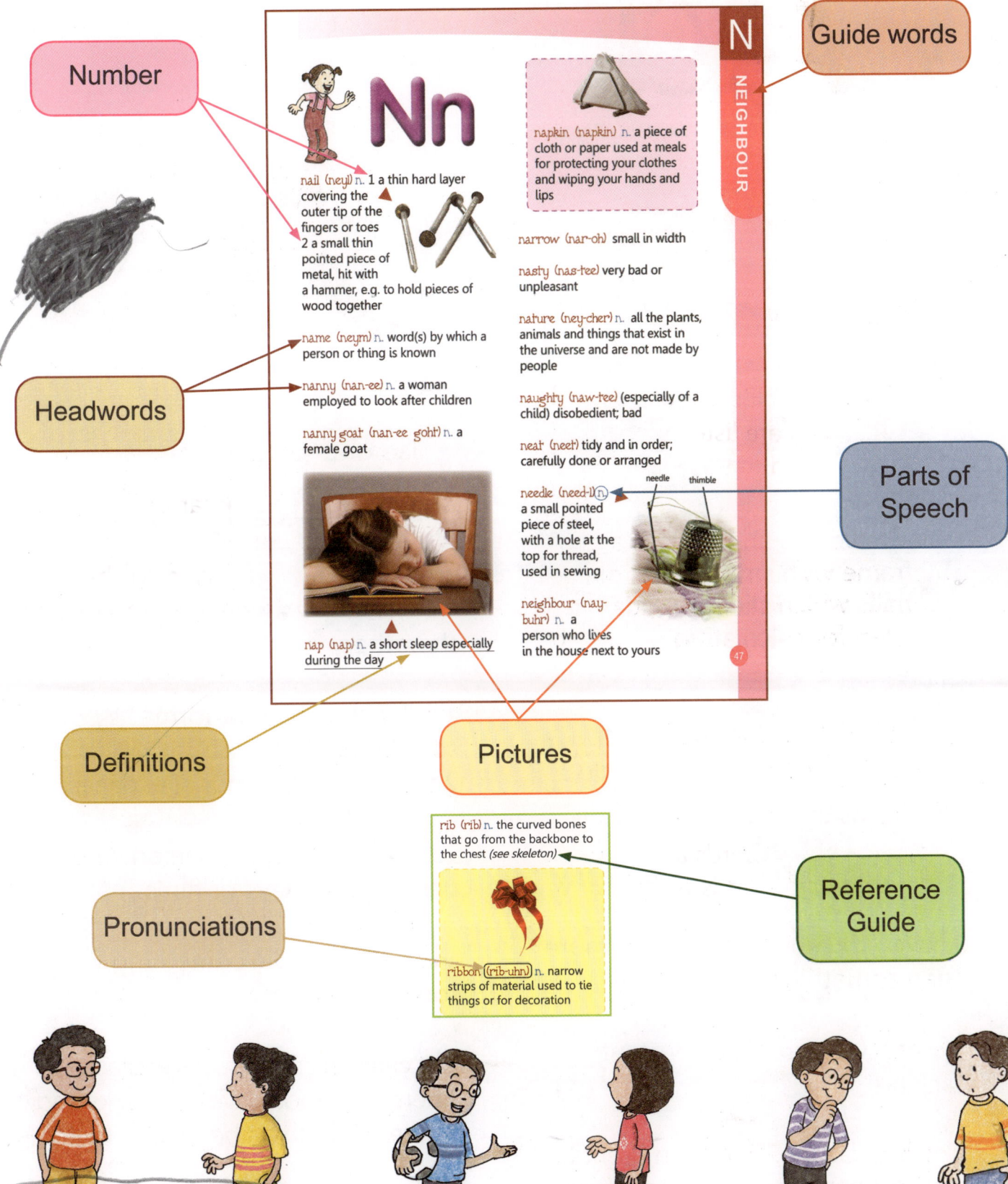

Aa

abacus (ab-uh-kuhs) n. a frame with small beads or balls which slide on rods, used for calculating

able (ey-bul) having the power, resources, or opportunity to do something

about (uh-bout) relating to; nearly

above (uh-buhv) higher than; more than something; greater than

absent (ab-suhnt) not present, lacking

accident (ak-si-duhnt) n. an event that occurs unexpectedly, especially one causing injury or harm

ache (eyk) v. to feel a steady and dull pain

acorn (ey-kawrn) n. fruit of the oak tree

acrobat (ak-ruh-bat) n. a person skilled at physical feats, especially gymnastics

across (uh-kraws) from one side to the other

act (akt) v. 1 to perform something; behave 2 to enact a role in a play or film

actor (ak-tuhr) n. a person who performs in plays or films

add (ad) v. to join something with something else

address (uh-dress) n. particulars of where somebody lives or works and where mailers can be posted to

admire (ad-mah-yuhr) v. to like someone or something

adventure (ad-ven-chuhr) n. an exciting, daring or dangerous journey or experience

aeroplane (air-uh-pleyn) n. a flying vehicle with fixed wings and one or more engines

afraid (uh-frayd) to be scared of somebody or something

afternoon (af-tuhr-noon) n. part of the day from 12 midday to evening

again (uh-gen) once more; another time

age (ayj) n. 1 a period of time somebody has lived or something has existed
2 the state of being old

agree (uh-gree) v. to have the same opinion or view as somebody

aid (eyd) n. to help

aim (eym) v. 1 to direct your efforts at achieving something
2 point a weapon or object towards something

air (air) n. 1 an invisible mixture of gases that we breathe
2 the earth's atmosphere

alert (uh-lurt) to be fully attentive and ready to act

alike (uh-like) in a similar way

alive (uh-live) living; having life

all (awl) the whole of a thing or of a period of time

alligator (al-ug-gayt-uhr) n. a large reptile of the crocodile family found in rivers and lakes in America and China

allow (uh-lou) v. to let something be done

alone (uh-lohn) without other people

aloud (uh-loud) to talk in a voice loud enough to be heard

alphabet (al-fuh-bet) n. a set of letters arranged in order, used to write a language

A
ALPHABET

altogether (awl-tuh-geth-er) completely, on the whole; including everything

always (awl-wayz) at all times; forever

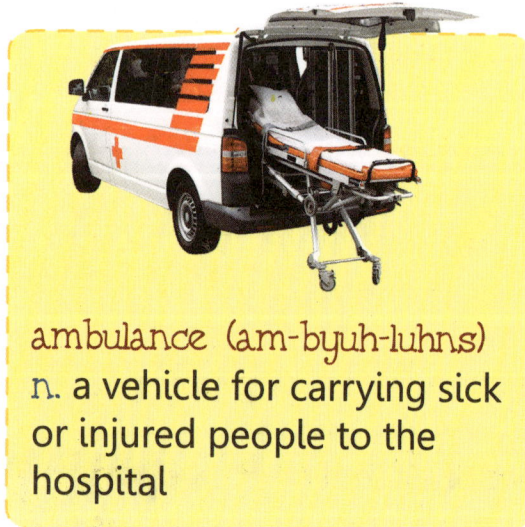

ambulance (am-byuh-luhns) n. a vehicle for carrying sick or injured people to the hospital

anchor (ang-ker) n. a heavy metal object lowered from a ship into the water in order to stop the ship from moving

anger (ang-ger) n. a feeling of extreme displeasure that makes people want to quarrel or fight

animal (an-uh-muhl) n. any living being that is not a plant

annoy (uh-noi) v. to make somebody slightly angry; to cause trouble to somebody

answer (an-suhr) n. something said or written in response to somebody or something; reply

ant (ant) n. a small insect that lives in organized groups

antelope (an-tl-ohp) n. a deer-like animal with long horns

any (en-ee) 1 some amount (of); one, some or all
2 no matter which

ape (ayp) n. a large animal like a monkey, with no tail, e.g. chimpanzee or gorilla

apple (ap-uhl) n. a round fruit with red or green skin and white flesh

apron (ey-pruh-n) n. a garment worn round the front part of your body to keep your clothes clean, e.g. when cooking

aquarium (uh-kwair-ee-uhm) n. a building with a large glass tank for keeping live fish and other water creatures

arithmetic (uh-rith-muh-tik) n. a branch of mathematics that deals with the adding, subtracting, multiplying and division of numbers

arm (ahrm) n. either of the two upper limbs of your body connecting the shoulder to the hand

army (ahr-mee) n. military forces of a country equipped to fight on land

arrive (uh-rive) v. to reach a place

arrow (ar-oh) n. a pointed stick shot from a bow

art (ahrt) n. making beautiful things like drawing, painting and many other activities

ask (ask) v. to request

asleep (uh-sleep) in a state of sleep; sleeping

athlete (ath-leet) n. a person trained for physical games

atlas (at-luhs) n. a book of maps

attention (uh-ten-shuhn) n. 1 careful thought 2 interest in somebody or something

autumn (awt-uhm) n. the season of the year between summer and winter

avoid (uh-void) v. to prevent something bad from happening

awake (uh-wayk) not asleep

away (uh-way) 1 to be at a distance from something 2 not present

awful (aw-fuhl) very bad or unpleasant

Bb

baby (bay-bee) n. a very young child or animal

back (bak) n. 1 the rear part of a body between the neck and the bottom
2 the part that is furthest from the front

backward (bak-wuhrd) 1 directed towards the back
2 less advanced; behind in development

backwards (bak-wuhrdz) 1 towards a place or position that is behind
2 with the back or end first

badge (baj) n. something worn to show membership, rank or office

badminton (bad-min-tn) n. a game like tennis, played by hitting a shuttlecock across a high net

bag (bag) n. a flexible container with an opening at the top

bake (bayk) v. to cook something in an oven

balance (bal-uhns) v. to put your body or something else into a position where it is steady and does not fall

ball (bawl) n. 1 a round object used in games
2 a large formal party with dancing

ballet (ba-lay) n. a style of dancing that tells a story with music but no talking or singing

balloon (buh-loon) n. a brightly coloured rubber bag filled with air

banana (buh-nan-uh) n. a long, yellow tropical fruit

bank (bangk) n. 1 a place where money is kept safely
2 land sloping up beside a river or lake

bark (bahrk) n. a short loud sound made by a dog

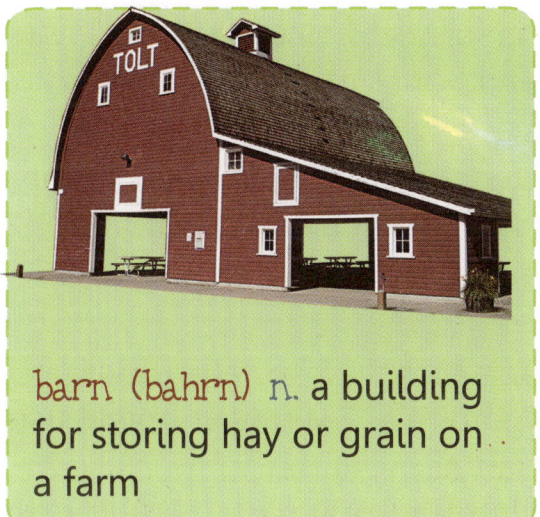

barn (bahrn) n. a building for storing hay or grain on a farm

basket (baskit) n. a container made of woven strips of cane or wire

bat (bat) n. a piece of wood with a handle for hitting the ball in cricket or baseball

bath (bath) n. a large container filled with water in which you sit to wash your body

beach (beech) n. a shore covered by sand or small stones

beat (beet) to defeat somebody; to be better than something

2 repeated stroke or hit
3 rhythm in music or poetry

beautiful (byoot-i-fuhl) very pretty or attractive

bed (bed) n. a piece of furniture that you sleep on

bee (bee) n. a black and yellow stinging insect that makes honey

begin (bi-gin) v. to start

behave (bih-heyv) v. to act in a particular way

behind (bi-hinde) 1 at, in, or to the back of somebody or something
2 making less progress than somebody or something

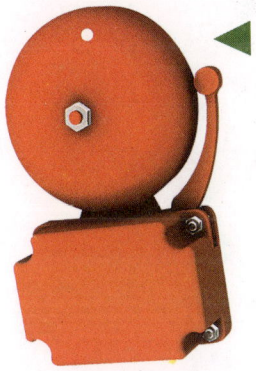 **bell** (bel) n. a metal object that makes a ringing sound when struck

belong (bi-lawng) v. to be owned by somebody

bench (bench) n. a long wooden or metal seat for two or more people

best (best) n. the most excellent thing or person

BICYCLE

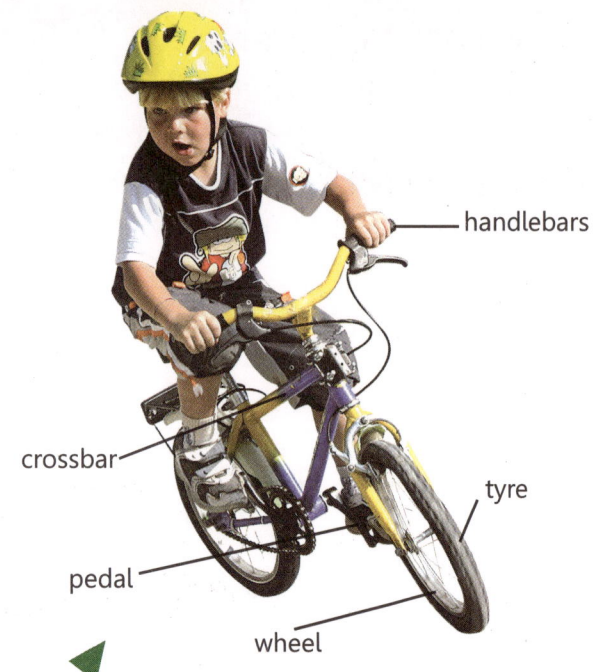

- handlebars
- crossbar
- pedal
- tyre
- wheel

bicycle (bie-sik-uhl) n. a road vehicle with two wheels that you ride by pushing the pedals with your feet

big (big) large in size, amount or importance

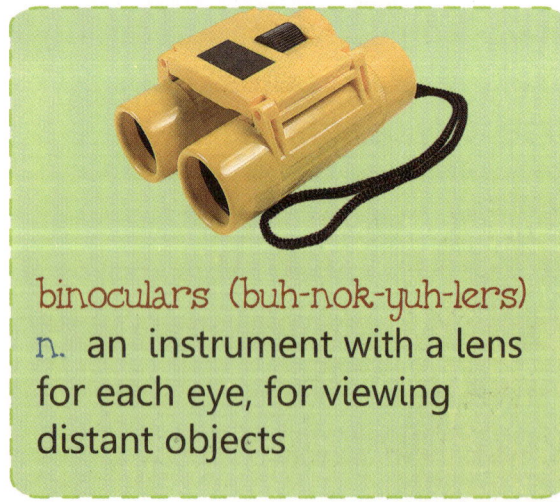

binoculars (buh-nok-yuh-lers) n. an instrument with a lens for each eye, for viewing distant objects

bird (buhrd) n. a creature with feathers and wings

blanket (blang-kit) n. a piece of thick cloth used as a warm covering on a bed

bleat (bleet) n. the sound of a sheep or goat

blind (blinde) 1 unable to see 2 a roll of cloth pulled down to cover a window

blow (bloh) v. to send out air from the mouth

boast (bohst) v. to talk about your own abilities, achievements or possessions with too much pride

boat (boht) n. a vehicle for travelling on water

bobsleigh (bob-sley) n. a sledge for racing on snow

body (bod-ee) n. the whole physical structure of a person or an animal

boil (boil) v. 1 to heat liquid till it is very hot that it gives off steam 2 to cook something in boiling water

book (buk) n. a number of printed sheets of paper fastened together in a cover

boot (boot) n. a shoe that covers the foot and ankle, and sometimes also the lower leg

bore (bohr) v. to make somebody feel tired and uninterested especially by talking too much

born (born) v. to come out of your mother's body at the beginning of your life

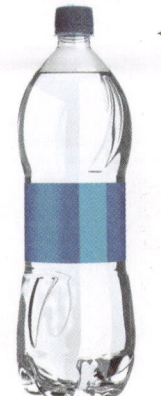

bottle (baht-l) n. a container with a narrow neck, for storing liquids

bough (bou) n. a large branch of a tree

bounce (bouns) v. to move quickly back from a surface that an object has just hit

bow (boh) v. to bend your head or the upper part of your body forward as a sign of respect or as a greeting

box (bahks) n. a container made of wood, cardboard, straw or tin usually with a lid, used for holding solid things

boy (boi) n. a male child; young man

brain (brayn) n. 1 an organ in the body that controls all the activities of the body
2 mind; intelligence

brave (brayv) to be willing to do things that are dangerous or painful; not afraid

break (brayk) v. to cause something to be damaged and separated into pieces

breakfast (brek-fuhst) n. the first meal of the day

bridge (brij) n. structure providing a way across a river, road, etc

bring (bring) v. to fetch, carry, or take something with you

B
BRUSH

brush (brush) n. a tool with bristles for cleaning and painting

bubble (buhb-uhl) n. a floating ball of liquid containing air or gas

bud (buhd) n. a flower or leaf before it opens

build (bild) v. make something by putting parts, etc together

bun (buhn) n. a small, round, sweet cake

bunny (buhn-ee) n. a child's word for a rabbit

burglar (bur-gler) n. a person who breaks into a building to steal things

bus (buhs) n. a large motor vehicle that carries passengers

butterfly (buht-ur-flie) n. an insect with a long, thin body and two pairs of large colourful wings

button (buht-n) n. a small round piece of metal or plastic that is sewn onto a piece of clothing as a fastener

buy (bie) v. get something by paying money for it

Cc

cab (kab) n. taxi

cabin (kab-uhn) n. 1 a small room or compartment in a ship or an aircraft
2 a small wooden shelter or hut

cage (kayj) n. a structure of bars or wires in which birds or animals are housed

call (kawl) v. 1 to give somebody or something a name
2 to say something loudly; shout
3 to telephone somebody

calm (kahm) not excited, nervous, or upset

camp (kamp) n. a place where people live in tents or huts temporarily usually to spend their holidays

candle (kan-duhl) n. a stick of wax with a string (wick) through it, which gives out light when it burns

canoe (kuh-noo) n. a light narrow boat which you propel along in the water with a paddle

cap (kap) n. 1 a soft, flat hat with a peak
2 the top covering, e.g. on a bottle or a tube of toothpaste

car (kahr) n. a motor vehicle for carrying passengers

card (kahrd) n. a thick, stiff paper with words, pictures, numbers or information on it

cartoon (kahr-toon) n. amusing drawings or a series of drawings in a newspaper or magazine

casket (kas-kit) n. a small box for holding jewellery or other valuable objects

C

castle (kas-uhl) n. an old, large building with thick walls, used for protection from enemies

caterpillar (kat-uhr-pil-uhr) n. a small creature like a worm with legs, which develops into a butterfly or moth

cave (kayv) n. a large hole in the side of a hill, or under the ground

cent (sent) n. one 100th part of a main unit of money, e.g. a dollar

cereal (sir-ee-uhl) n. edible grain produced by a kind of grass, e.g. wheat or maize

champion (cham-pee-uhn) n. a person or team that wins a competition

change (chaynj) v. to become or make somebody or something different

chase (chays) v. to run or drive after somebody in order to catch them or make them go away

chat (chat) n. friendly, informal talk

cheese (cheez) n. solid food made from milk

cherry (cher-ee) n. a small, round, red or black fruit with a stone inside

chew (choo) v. to bite food into small pieces in your mouth with your teeth

child (childe) n. 1 a young human being 2 son or daughter of any age

chimney (chim-nee) n. a structure through which smoke is carried away from a fire and through the roof of a building

chirp (churp) v. make the short, sharp sound of small birds

chocolate (chahk-luht) n. hard, brown sweet food made from cocoa beans

choose (chooz) v. to decide which thing or person you want from a number of available alternatives

chubby (chuhb-ee) slightly fat

cinema (sin-uh-muh) n. a place where films are shown

circle (suhr-kuhl) n. a curved line where every point is the same distance from the centre; a ring

circus (suhr-kuhs) n. a group of entertainers, sometimes with trained animals, who perform in a show that travel around to different places

city (sit-ee) n. a large, important town

clap (klap) v. to hit your open hands together several times to show your approval or appreciation of something

class (klas) n. group of students taught together

claw (klaw) n. a hard, curved nail at the end of the foot of an animal or a bird

clean (kleen) not dirty

clever (klev-er) quick at learning and understanding; intelligent

climate (klahy-mit) n. the general weather conditions of a place

climb (klime) v. to go up something, especially using both hands and feet

clock (klahk) n. an instrument for measuring and showing the time

close (klohs) v. to cause something to shut

clothes (klohz) n. things that you wear like trousers and dresses

cloud (kloud) n. a mass of visible water vapour floating in the sky

clown (kloun) n. a performer in a circus who does silly things to make people laugh

clumsy (kluhm-zee) lacking in skill and ungraceful in movement

coat (koht) n. a piece of clothing worn over other clothes to keep warm

cobweb (kob-web) n. a spider's home

coin (koin) n. piece of metal used as money

cold (kohld) 1 not warm or hot 2 common illness of the nose or throat

collect (kuh-lekt) v. come together; bring together

colour (kuhl-uhr) n. when light meets the eyes, it produces colours; red, blue and yellow are colours

comb (kohm) n. a piece of plastic or metal with teeth used for tidying your hair

compass (kuhm-puhs) n. a device for finding direction with a needle that points north

compete (kuhm-peet) v. to take part in a race or contest; try to win by defeating others

concert (kahn-suhrt) n. a musical performance

contest (kahn-test) n. a fight; competition

continent (kahnt-n-uhnt) n. one of the main land masses

cook (kuk) v. to prepare food by boiling, baking or frying

corn (korn) n. 1 the grain of any plant that is grown for its grain, such as wheat and oat 2 maize

cot (kot) n. a small bed for a young child

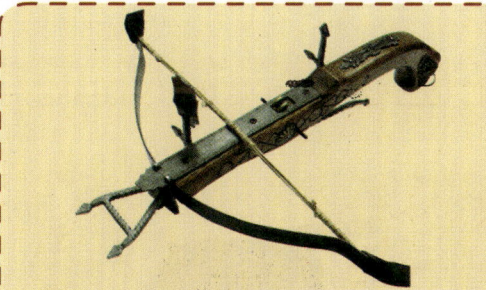

couch (kouch) n. a long comfortable seat like a bed

craft (kraft) n. an activity needing skill at making things with your hands

crayon (kray-uhn) n. a pencil of soft coloured chalk or wax used for drawing and clouring

crossbow (kraws-boh) n. a weapon consisting of a bow that is fixed onto a larger piece of wood, and that shoots short, heavy arrows

cry (krie) v. to produce tears from the eyes because you are unhappy or hurt

cup (kuhb) n. a small bowl with a handle for drinking tea and coffee

cupboard (kuhb-erd) n. a set of shelves with doors in the front

curtain (kur-tn) n. a piece of cloth, hung up to cover a window or divide a room

curve (kurv) n. a line or surface that bends gradually; smooth bend

cushion (koosh-uhn) n. a small bag filled with soft material, to make a seat more comfortable

custard (kuhs-terd) n. a sweet yellow sauce made from eggs, sugar, flour and milk

cut (kuht) v. to make an opening or wound in something with something sharp

cycle (sahy-kuhl) n. a bicycle or motorcycle *(see bicycle)*

Dd

dab (dab) v. to touch something lightly or gently

daily (dey-lee) happening or appearing every day or every weekday

dairy (dair-ee) n. a building on a farm where butter and cheese are made

daisy (dey-zee) n. a small flower with a yellow centre and white petals

dam (dam) n. a wall built to keep back water

damage (dam-ij) v. harm or spoil somebody or something

dark (dark) with no or very little light

dash (dash) v. to go somewhere quickly

date (dayt) n. the particular day of the month or year

dead (ded) of people, animals or plants no longer alive

deaf (def) unable to hear

deep (deep) going a long way down from the top or surface

defend (dih-fend) v. to protect somebody or something from attack

delicious (dih-lish-uhs) having a very pleasant taste or smell

delight (dih-lahyt) n. great pleasure

den (den) n. a wild animal's hidden home

desert (dez-uhrt) n. a large area of land, without water and trees, often covered with sand

desk (desk) n. a table, usually with drawers in it, that you sit at to read, write, or work

diary (dahy-uh-ree) n. a book used for a daily record of events or future appointments

◄ **dice** (dahys) n. a small cube marked with spots to indicate numbers used in games

dictionary (dik-shuh-ner-ee) n. a book containing the words of a language, with their meanings, arranged in alphabetical order

different (dif-ruhnt) not the same

difficult (dif-uh-kuhlt) not easy

dig (dig) v. to make a hole in the ground

dinner (din-uhr) n. the main meal of the day, eaten either at midday or in the evening

dinosaur (die-nuh-sor) n. a large prehistoric reptile that no longer exists

dip (dip) v. to put something into a liquid for a short time

dirt (duhrt) n. unclean matter, e.g. dust or mud

discover (dis-kuh-vuhr) v. to find or learn about something for the first time

dish (dish) n. a flat shallow container for cooking or serving food ►

disobey (dis-uh-bey) v. to refuse to do what you are told to do

disturb (dih-sturb) v. to interrupt somebody

D

DISTURB

D

dive (dive) v. to go under water with the head entering first

divide (duh-vide) v. to separate; break something into parts

dizzy (diz-ee) feeling as if everything is turning round and round; unable to balance

◀ **doll** (dahl) n. a child's toy in the shape of a person, especially a baby or a child

doodle (dood-l) v. to do small drawings while you are thinking about something else

door (dor) n. a piece of wood used for closing the entrance to a building or room

▲ **dozen** (duhz-uhn) n. a set of twelve of the same thing

drag (drag) v. to pull somebody or something along with effort and difficulty

dragon (drag-uhn) n. (in stories and myths) a large animal with wings and claws, able to breathe out fire

draw (draw) v. to make a picture with a pen or pencil

drawer (dror) n. a box-like container that slides in and out of a desk or chest

drink (dringk) v. to take liquid into your mouth and swallow it

drop (drahp) v. to fall or allow something to fall

drum (druhm) n. ▶ musical instrument made of skin stretched tightly across a hollow round frame

dry (drie) not wet

dumb (duhm) unable to speak

dwarf (dwawrf) n. a person, animal, or plant that is much smaller than usual

Ee

eagle (ee-guhl) n. a large strong bird that eats small animals

ear (ir) n. part of the body on each side of the head used for hearing

early (uhr-lee) 1 near to the beginning of something 2 before the usual or expected time

earth (uhrth) n. 1 (the Earth) the world; the planet we live in 2 the surface of the world; land

easy (ee-zee) 1 not difficult 2 free from anxiety, pain, or trouble

eat (eet) v. to put food into your mouth and swallow it

educate (ej-oo-keet) v. to teach somebody

elbow (el-boh) n. joint where the arm bends

elf (elf) n. (in stories) a creature with pointed ears and magic powers

empty (emp-tee) containing nothing or no one

enjoy (en-joi) v. to get pleasure from something

enough (i-nuhf) as many or as much as somebody needs or wants

enter (ent-uhr) v. to come or go into something

E

ENTER

E

ENVELOPE

envelope (en-vel-uhp) n. a paper covering for a letter

evening (eev-ning) n. part of the day between the afternoon and bedtime

evergreen (ev-er-green) n. that has green leaves throughout the year

every (ev-ree) each one; all

evil (eev-il) wicked; cruel

example (ig-zam-puhl) n. a fact or thing that shows a general rule or represents a group

exercise (ek-suhr-size) n. a physical or mental activity that keeps you healthy

explode (ik-splohd) v. to burst loudly and violently, usually causing damage

extra (ek-struh) more than usual or necessary; additional

Ff

face (fays) n. the front part of the head

faint (feynt) 1 that cannot be clearly seen, heard, or smelt 2 to be weak and lose your senses

fairy (fair-ee) n. a small imaginary creature with magical powers

family (fam-uh-lee) n. 1 a group consisting of one or two parents and their children 2 a group consisting of one or two parents, their children and close relations

famous (fey-muhs) known about by many people

farm (fahrm) n. the area of land and buildings for growing crops and raising animals

fast (fast) quick

favourite (fay-vuh-rit) n. a person or thing liked more than others

feather (feth-uhr) n. one of the many light parts that cover a bird's body

feed (feed) v. to give food to somebody or something

feel (feel) v. to touch

find (finde) v. to discover something or somebody unexpectedly

flee (flee) v. to run or hurry away from somebody or something; to escape

flour (flour) n. a fine powder made from grain, used for making bread and cake

flow (floh) v. to move steadily and continuously

FLOWER

sun flower   geranium   rose

flower (flou-uhr) n. part of a plant that produces seeds, often brightly coloured

flute (floot) n. a musical instrument like a thin pipe, played by blowing across a hole at one end

fly (flahy) v. 1 to move through the air as a bird does or an aircraft 2 an insect with two wings

follow (fahl-oh) v. to come or go after somebody or something

fond (fond) having a great liking for somebody or something

food (food) n. 1 things that people or animals eat 2 a particular kind of food

forest (for-ist) n. a large area of land covered with trees

fork (fawrk) n.
1 a tool with sharp points, used for lifting food to the mouth
2 a gardening tool with metal points, used for digging

gardening fork

fountain (foun-tn) n. an ornamental structure from which water is pumped into the air

friend (frend) n. a person you know well and like, but who is not a relative

front (fruhnt) n. 1 part or side of something that faces forward 2 the part of somebody's body that faces forward; the chest

frown (froun) v. to bring your eyebrows together to express anger, displeasure or thought

fruit (froot) n. part of a plant used as food, e.g. orange, banana

fry (frie) v. to cook something in hot fat or oil

fuel (fyoo-uhl) n. material, e.g. coal or oil, burned to produce heat or power

full (fool) 1 holding as much or as many as possible 2 having eaten enough

fun (fuhn) n. as enjoyment; pleasure

funny (fuhn-ee) causing laughter; amusing

fur (fuhr) n. the soft, thick hair covering a cat, beaver, rabbit and many other animals

furniture (fur-ni-cher) n. large movable things, e.g. sofas, chairs, etc in a house or office

further (fur-ther) at or to a greater distance in space or time

fuss (fuhs) n. unnecessary excitement, worry, or activity

F
FUSS

Gg

garage (guh-rahj) n. 1 a room in a house in which a car is kept *(see house)* 2 a place where cars are repaired

garbage (gahr-bij) n. rubbish

garden (gahrd-n) n. a piece of land next to or around your house used for growing flowers and vegetables *(see house)*

garland (gahr-luhnd) n. a circle of flowers or leaves used as a decoration.

gate (gayt) n. a movable barrier that closes an opening in a wall, fence, etc

gaze (geyz) v. to look steadily at somebody or something for a long time

gentle (jent-l) not rough or violent

giant (jie-uhnt) n. (in stories) an enormous and very strong person

gift (gift) n. something given freely; a present

gill (gil) n. an organ through which a fish breathes

girl (guhrl) n. a female child; daughter; young woman

glad (glad) pleased; happy

glass (glahs) n. 1 a hard, transparent substance used in windows and mirrors 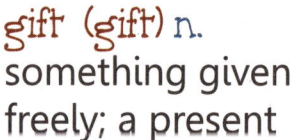 2 a drinking container made of glass; its contents

glee (glee) n. a feeling of happiness and satisfaction

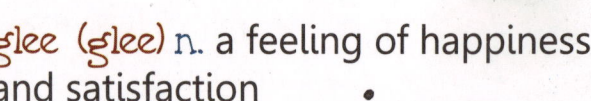

G

globe (glohb) n. a model of the earth

group (groop) n. a number of people or things together

glove (gluhv) n. a covering for the hand

glue (gloo) n. a sticky substance used for joining things together

grass (gras) n. common, wild, short green plant eaten by cattle

great (grayt) very large in size, quantity, or degree

greed (greed) n. a strong desire for too much food or money

greet (greet) v. to say hello to somebody or welcome somebody

grin (grin) v. to smile widely

ground (ground) n. the solid surface of the earth

grow (groh) v. to increase in size, number, strength, or quality

guess (ges) v. to try and give an answer or form an opinion about something without being sure of all the facts

gulp (guhlp) v. to swallow food or drink quickly

gum (guhm) n. either of the firm areas of pink flesh around the teeth

exercise bike

treadmill

punching bag

gym (jim) n. room or hall with equipment for physical exercise

GYM

29

Hh

habit (hab-it) n. a thing that you do often and almost without thinking because you are used to doing it

hair (hair) n. substance that looks like a mass of fine threads growing especially on the head

half (haf) n. one of two equal parts

hammer (ham-uhr) n. a tool with a heavy metal head, used for hitting nails

handshake (hand-sheyk) v. shaking somebody's hand with your own, as a greeting

happy (hap-ee) feeling, giving or expressing pleasure; pleased

harbour (hahr-buhr) n. a place of shelter for ships

hard (hahrd) 1 firm and solid; not easy to bend or cut 2 difficult

harmony (hahr-muh-nee) n. a state of peaceful existence and agreement

hat (hat) n. a covering for the head

hate (hayt) v. to have a great dislike for somebody or something

heal (heel) v. to become or make something healthy again

health (helth) n. the state of being physically and mentally healthy

hear (heer) v. to be aware of sounds with your ears

heart (hahrt) n. an organ that pumps blood around the body

heavy (hev-ee) weighing a lot; difficult to lift or move

helmet (hel-mit) n. a protective covering for the head

help (help) v. to do part of the work of somebody; be of use or service to somebody; to aid someone

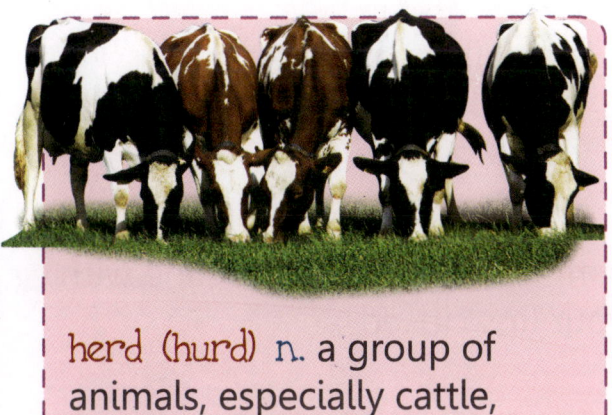

herd (hurd) n. a group of animals, especially cattle, together

hero (hir-oh) n. a person admired for bravery or other good qualities

hiccup (hik-uhp) n. a sudden repeated stopping of the breath with a sound that you cannot control

hide (hide) v. to put or keep somebody or something out of sight

hill (hil) n. an area of high land, not as high as a mountain

hit (hit) v. bring something forcefully against somebody or something

hive (hive) n. a box for bees to live in

hobby (hob-ee) n. an activity you do for pleasure in your free time

hold (hohld) v. to carry something; have somebody or something in your hands

home (hohm) n. a place where you live, especially with your family

honey (huhn-ee) n. sweet sticky substance made by bees

hop (hahp) n. a short jump with both feet

hope (hohp) n. the desire and expectation that something good will happen

H

horrid (hawr-id) very unpleasant; nasty

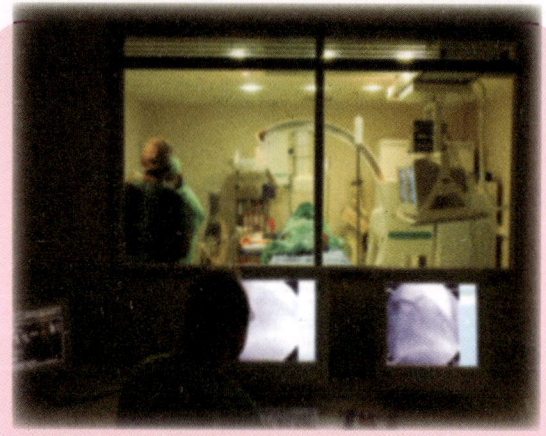

hospital (hahs-pit-l) n. a place where people are treated for illness or injuries

host (hohst) n. a person who entertains guests in their house

hostel (hos-tl) n. a building providing cheap accommodation for students, travellers, etc

hour (our) n. a period of 60 minutes

house (hous) n. a building made for people to live in, usually for one family

hug (huhg) v. put your arms round somebody tightly, especially to show love

huge (hyooj) very large

hush (huhsh) v. become or make somebody or something quiet

hum (huhm) v. to sing a tune with your lips closed

hurt (huhrt) v. to cause injury or pain to somebody or yourself

hut (huht) n. a small roughly built house or shelter

hutch (huhch) n. a cage for rabbits, etc

hygiene (hahy-jeen) n. keeping yourself and your living area clean, in order to prevent disease

Ii

ice (ise) n. water that has frozen and has become solid

igloo (ig-loo) n. a small round house made of blocks of snow

ill (il) sick; suffering from an illness or disease

inject (in-jekt) v. to put something into somebody with a syringe

injure (in-jer) v. hurt or damage somebody or something

ink (ingk) n. coloured liquid for writing

instead (in-sted) in the place of somebody or something

instrument (in-struh-muhnt) n. a tool or device used for a particular task, especially delicate or scientific work

interest (in-ter-ist) n. the desire to learn or know about somebody or something

introduce (in-truh-doos) v. to make somebody known to somebody else by giving each person's name to the other

invite (in-vite) v. to ask somebody to go somewhere or to do something

iron (ie-uhrn) n. a hard strong metal, used in manufacturing and building

island (ie-luhnd) n. a piece of land surrounded by water

itch (ich) n. a feeling of irritation on the skin, causing a desire to scratch

ivy (ahy-vee) n. a climbing evergreen plant with dark shiny leaves

Jj

jab (jab) v. to push a pointed object into somebody or something with sudden force

jacket (jak-it) n. a short coat with sleeves

jail (jayl) n. prison

jam (jam) n. sweet food made by boiling fruit with sugar, eaten on bread

jar (jahr) n. a round glass container with a lid, used for storing food

jaw (jaw) n. either of the bone structures containing the teeth

jeans (jeenz) n. trousers made of strong cotton, especially denim

jeep (jeep) n. a motor vehicle for driving over rough ground

jelly (jel-ee) n. clear sweet soft fruit-flavoured food

jet (jet) n. an aircraft powered by a jet engine

jewel (joo-uhl) n. a precious stone, e.g. a diamond

jigsaw (jig-saw) n. cardboard or wood cut into irregular shapes that has to be fitted together again

job (job) n. work for which you receive regular payment

jockey (jok-ee) n. a professional rider in horse races

jog (jahg) v. to run slowly especially for exercise

join (join) v. to fix or connect two or more things together

joint (joint) n. the place where two bones are joined together

joke (johk) n. something said or done to make people laugh

jolly (jol-ee) happy and cheerful

jot (jot) v. to write something quickly

joy (joi) n. great happiness

jug (juhg) n. a deep container for liquids, with a handle and a lip

juggle (juhg-uhl) v. to keep objects, especially balls, in the air by throwing and catching them

juice (joos) n. liquid obtained from fruit, vegetables or meat

jump (juhmp) v. to move quickly off the ground by pushing yourself with your legs and feet

jungle (juhng-ghul) n. land in a tropical country, covered with thick forest

junior (joon-yer) 1 lower in rank than somebody
2 (Junior) used after the name of a man who has the same name as his father

junk (juhngk) n. old or unwanted things, usually of little value

just (juhst) 1 exactly
2 no less than; equally

J

JUST

Kk

karate (kuh-rah-tee) n. a system of fighting, using the hands and feet

keep (keep) v. to hold something in a given place or for sometime

kennel (ken-l) n. a small shelter for a dog

ketchup (kech-uhp) n. thick cold sauce made from tomatoes

kettle (ket-l) n. a container with a spout, used for boiling water

key (kee) n. a piece of metal that locks or unlocks a door or box

kick (kik) v. to hit somebody or something with your foot

kid (kid) n. 1 a child or young person 2 the young one of a goat

kidnap (kid-nap) v. to take somebody away illegally and keep them prisoner, especially in order to demand money

kidney (kid-nee) n. an organ that removes waste products from the blood and produces urine

kind (kinde) being friendly and thoughtful to others

king (king) n. the male ruler of an independent state that has a royal family

kingdom (king-duhm) n. a country, state or territory ruled by a king or queen.

kiss (kis) v. to touch somebody with your lips to show affection or as a greeting

kitchen (kich-uhn) n. a room or place in the house where meals are cooked

kite (kite) n. a toy consisting of a light framework covered with paper or cloth which flies in the wind

kitten (kit-n) n. the young of a cat

knife (nife) n. a sharp blade with a handle, used for cutting

knight (nite) n. (in the Middle Ages) a soldier of noble birth

knit (nit) v. to make clothes, from wool or cotton thread using two long needles

knock (nok) v. to hit a door firmly to attract attention

knot (not) n. a fastening made by tying together pieces of string or rope

know (noh) v. 1 to have information in your mind about something
2 to realize, understand or be aware of something

knowledge (nol-ij) n. information, understanding and skills gained through education or experience

knuckle (nuhk-uhl) n. any of the joints in the fingers

koala (koh-ah-luh) n. an Australian tree-climbing animal like a small bear

Ll

lack (lak) v. to have none or not enough of something

ladder (lad-uhr) n. two lengths of wood or metal, joined together with steps or rungs, used for climbing

lady (ley-dee) n. a woman who has good manners

lake (leyk) n. a large area of water surrounded by land

lame (leym) unable to walk well because of injury to the leg or foot

lamp (lamp) n. a device that uses electricity, oil or gas to produce light

land (land) n. solid dry part of the earth's surface

lane (leyn) n. a narrow country road or street

language (lang-gwij) n. a mode which people use through words to talk and understand each other

lap (lap) n. the top part of your legs that forms a flat surface when you sit down

laugh (laf) v. to make the sounds and movements of your face that show you are happy or think something is funny

lazy (lay-zee) unwilling to work

lead (leed) v. to go with or in front of a person or an animal to show the way

leaf (leef) n. one of the usually green and flat parts of a plant growing from a stem

leap (leep) v. to jump high or a long way

learn (luhrn) v. to gain knowledge or skill in a subject or activity

letter (let-uhr) n. a written message sent to somebody

leather (leth-uhr) n. a material from animal skins, used for making shoes, jackets and bags

library (lie-brer-ee) n. a room or building which has a collection of books or records

leave (leev) v. to go away from a person or place

lemon (lem-uhn) n. a yellow citrus fruit with a sour juice

lend (lend) v. to give the use of something to somebody for a short time

length (lengkth) n. the size or measurement of something from one end to the other

less (les) a smaller amount of

lesson (les-uhn) n. a period of time in which somebody is taught something

let (let) v. to allow somebody to do something or something to happen

lie (lie) v. to say or write something that you know is not true

life (life) n. the ability to breathe, grow and reproduce which makes people, animals and plants different from objects

lift (lift) v. to raise somebody or something or be raised to a higher level or position

light (lite) n. energy from the sun or a lamp that makes it possible to see things

like (like) 1 to find somebody or something pleasant, attractive or satisfactory; enjoy something 2 similar to somebody or something

line (line) n. a long thin mark on a surface

list (list) n. a set of names or things written down in order

litter (lit-er) n. 1 a number of young animals born at the same time
2 bits of paper, bottles, etc that people have left lying in a public place

little (lit-l) 1 small 2 young 3 (of distance or time) short

live (liv) living; not dead

load (lohd) n. a thing that is carried by a person or vehicle

loaf (lohf) n. a mass of shaped and baked bread

lock (lok) n. a device for fastening a door

locker (lok-er) n. small cupboards that can be locked, used for storing things especially found in schools

locket (lok-it) n. a piece of jewellery, worn on a chain around the neck, in which you can keep a picture, piece of hair, etc.

log (lawg) n. a thick piece of wood that is cut from or has fallen from a tree

lollipop (lol-ee-pop) n. a large boiled sweet or piece of frozen fruit juice on a stick

lonely (lohn-lee) sad because you have no friends or people to talk to

long (lawng) 1 not short 2 to want something very much

look (look) v. to use your eyes to see something

loose (loos) not firmly fixed where it should be

lost (lawst) unable to find your way; not knowing where you are

lot (lot) n. 1 the whole number or amount of people or things 2 a group or set of people or things

loud (loud) making a lot of noise

love (luhv) n. a strong feeling of deep affection for somebody or something

luggage (luhg-ayj) n. bags, suitcases taken on a journey

lullaby (luhl-uh-bahy) n. a song sung to make a child go to sleep

lump (luhmp) n. something hard or solid, usually shapeless

lunch (luhnch) n. a meal eaten in the middle of the day

lung (luhng) n. either of the two breathing organs in the chest

Mm

MACHINE

machine (muh-sheen) n. a piece of equipment with moving parts that uses power to perform a particular task

mad (mad) 1 mentally ill 2 very stupid; crazy

magic (maj-ik) n. the art of doing tricks that seem impossible in order to entertain people

magnet (mag-nuht) n. a piece of iron that attracts other metal objects towards it

mail (mayl) n. letters and packages that are sent and delivered by post

main (meyn) being the largest or most important of its kind

maize (meyz) n. a tall plant grown for its large yellow grains that are used for making flour or eaten as a vegetable

major (mey-jer) very large or important

make (meyk) v. to construct, produce or prepare something; bring something into existence

mammal (mam-uhl) n. any animal that gives birth to live babies, not eggs, and feeds its young on milk

manage (man-ij) v. to succeed in doing something, especially something difficult

mane (meyn) n. long hair on the neck of a horse or lion

mango (mang-goh) n. a tropical fruit with soft orange flesh and a large seed inside

manner (man-er) n. a way in which something is done or happens

many (men-ee) a large number of people or things

map (map) n. a drawing or plan of the earth's surface, showing countries, towns, rivers and other features of the earth

marble (mahr-buhl) n. 1 a kind of hard stone, used, when cut and polished, for building and sculpture 2 a small ball of coloured glass that children roll along the ground in a game

market (mahr-kit) n. a place where people buy and sell goods

marry (mar-ee) v. to become the husband or wife of somebody

mask (mask) n. a covering for part or all of the face worn to hide or protect it

mason (mey-suhn) n. a person who builds in or works with stone

mat (mat) n. a piece of thick material or carpet used to cover part of a floor

match (mach) n. 1 a short piece of wood or cardboard used for lighting a fire 2 a sports event where people or teams compete against each other

mathematics (math-uh-mat-iks) n. the science of numbers and shapes

M

MATTRESS

mattress (mat-ris) n. the soft part of a bed, that you lie on

meadow (med-oh) n. a field of grass

measure (mezh-uhr) v. to find the size, length, degree and weight of an object or person

meat (meet) n. the flesh of animals, used as food

medal (med-l) n. a small round flat piece of metal, given as an honour for bravery or as a prize

medicine (med-uh-suhn) n. a substance, especially a liquid that is taken to cure an illness

meet (meet) v. come together with somebody

melt (melt) v. to cause something to become liquid as a result of heating

memory (mem-uh-ree) n. your ability to remember things

mend (mend) v. to repair something damaged or broken so that it can be used again

merry (mer-ee) happy and cheerful

middle (mid-l) n. the position at an equal distance from all the edges or between the beginning and the end of something

midnight (mid-nite) n. at 12 o'clock in the middle of the night

mild (mahyld) gentle; not severe

milk (milk) n. white liquid produced by female mammals as food for their young

mill (mil) n. a building with machinery for grinding grain into flour

44

mind (minde) n. part of a person's brain where your thoughts are

mind (minde) v. to be careful

mine (mine) of or belonging to me

mirror (mir-uhr) n. a piece of glass that you can look in and see yourself

misbehave (mis-bi-heyv) v. to behave badly

miss (mis) v. 1 fail to hit, catch or reach something 2 to feel sad because someone or something is not there

mistake (mi-steyk) n. a wrong action, idea or opinion

mitten (mit-n) n. a kind of glove that covers the four fingers together and the thumb separately

mix (miks) v. to cause two or more substances to combine, usually in a way that means they cannot easily be separated

modern (mod-ern) of the present or recent times

mole (mohl) n. a small grey furry animal that lives in tunnels

money (muh-nee) n. coins and printed paper accepted when buying and selling

monster (mon-ster) n. a large ugly frightening creature

mood (mood) n. the way you are feeling at a particular time

moon (moon) n. the round object that moves round the earth and shines at night

more (mor) to a greater extent than something else; to a greater degree than usual

morning (mor-ning) n. the early part of the day from the time when people wake up until midday or before lunch

mosquito (muh-skeet-oh) n. a small flying insect that sucks blood

M

MOSQUITO

M

mountain (moun-tuhn) n. a very high hill, often with rocks near the top

move (moov) v. to change place or position

mow (moh) v. to cut grass with a lawnmower

much (muhch) a large amount or quantity of something

mud (muhd) n. soft wet earth

mule (myool) n. an animal that is half donkey and half horse, used for carrying heavy loads

munch (muhnch) v. to eat something steadily and often noisily

muscle (muhs-il) n. an elastic tissue in the body that you tighten to produce movement

museum (myoo-zee-uhm) n. a building in which objects of art, history or science are shown

mushroom (muhsh-room) n. fungus of which some kinds can be eaten

music (myoo-zik) n. sounds arranged in a way that is pleasant or exciting to listen to

must (muhst) n. a thing that should be done or seen

mystery (mis-tuh-ree) n. something that cannot be understood or explained

Nn

napkin (napkin) n. a piece of cloth or paper used at meals for protecting your clothes and wiping your hands and lips

nail (neyl) n. 1 a thin hard layer covering the outer tip of the fingers or toes 2 a small thin pointed piece of metal, hit with a hammer, e.g. to hold pieces of wood together

name (neym) n. word(s) by which a person or thing is known

nanny (nan-ee) n. a woman employed to look after children

nanny goat (nan-ee goht) n. a female goat

narrow (nar-oh) small in width

nasty (nas-tee) very bad or unpleasant

nature (ney-cher) n. all the plants, animals and things that exist in the universe and are not made by people

naughty (naw-tee) (especially of a child) disobedient; bad

neat (neet) tidy and in order; carefully done or arranged

needle   thimble

needle (need-l) n. a small pointed piece of steel, with a hole at the top for thread, used in sewing

neighbour (nay-buhr) n. a person who lives in the house next to yours

nap (nap) n. a short sleep especially during the day

NEIGHBOUR

N

nest (nest) n. a home made by a bird to lay eggs

net (net) n. a loose open material made of knotted string or wire which is often used for catching fish

never (nev-uhr) not at any time; not on any occasion

new (noo) not existing before; recently made

night (nite) n. the time of darkness between one day and the next

nightingale (nahyt-n-geyl) n. a small bird that sings sweetly

nobody (noh-bod-ee) not anybody; no person

noise (noiz) n. a sound especially when loud or unpleasant

noun (noun) n. a word that refers to a person, a place, an animal or a thing

now (nou) at the present time

number (nuhm-ber) n. a symbol or word representing a quantity

nurse (nurs) n. a person whose job is to take care of ill or injured people, usually in a hospital

nursery (nur-suh-ree) n. 1 a place where young children are cared for while their parents are at work 2 a place where young plants are grown

nut (nuht) n. a small hard fruit with a hard shell that grows on some trees

Oo

oak (ohk) n. 1 a large tree that produces small nuts, often eaten by animals 2 the hard wood of the oak tree

oar (ohr) n. a long pole with a flat blade, used for rowing a boat

obey (oh-bay) v. to do what you are told or expected to do

object (ob-jekt) n. a thing that can be seen or touched but is not alive

occasion (uh-key-zhuhn) n. a special event or celebration

ocean (oh-shuhn) n. one of the very large areas of sea on the earth's surface

o'clock (uh-klahk) used with the numbers 1 to 12 when telling the time, to mean an exact hour

odour (oh-der) n. a smell

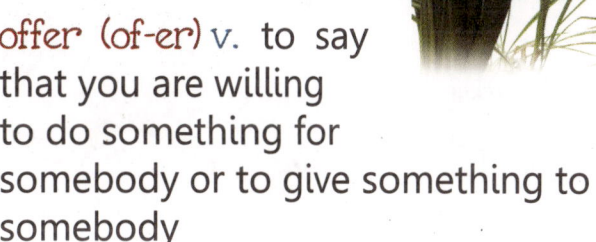

offer (of-er) v. to say that you are willing to do something for somebody or to give something to somebody

often (of-uhn) many times; frequently

oil (oil) n. a thick slippery liquid that burns easily used for fuel or cooking

old (ohld) having lived for a long time

only (ohn-lee) with no other(s) of the same group

open (oh-puhn) not closed

opposite (ahp-uh-zuht) as different as possible from something

orphan (awr-fuhn) n. a child whose parents are dead

ostrich (ahs-trich) n. a very large African bird with a long neck and long legs, that cannot fly

other (uhth-er) used to refer to a person or thing additional to that already mentioned

otherwise (uhth-er-wahyz) 1 used to state what the result would be if the situation were different 2 apart from that

our (ou-er) of or belonging to us

out (out) not at home or at a place of work

outdoor (out-doorz) done or situated outside rather than in a building

outfit (outfit) n. clothing or equipment needed for a particular occasion or purpose

outside (out-side) n. the outer side or surface of something

oval (oh-vuhl) n. shaped like an egg

oven (uhv-uhn) n. an enclosed box-like space in which food is cooked

over (oh-ver) resting on the surface of and partly or completely covering somebody or something

owl (oul) n. a bird of prey with large round eyes, that hunts at night

own (ohn) v. to possess something

oyster (oi-ster) n. a large flat shellfish

Pp

pack (pak) v. to put clothes into a bag for a trip away from home

packet (pak-it) n. a small container in which goods are packed for selling

paddle (pad-l) n. a short pole with a wide flat part at one or both ends, used to move a small boat through water

page (payj) n. one side or both sides of a sheet of paper in a book

pagoda (puh-goh-duh) n. a religious building in the form of a tower with several levels

pain (payn) n. feelings of suffering that you have in your body when you are hurt or ill

paint (paynt) n. coloured liquid that is put on a surface

pair (pair) n. two things of the same kind

palace (pal-uhs) n. a large splendid house especially the official home of a king, queen or president

palette (pal-it) n. a board on which an artist mixes colours

pan (pan) n. a metal container with a handle used for cooking

pancake (pan-kayk) n. a thin flat round cake of batter fried on both sides

paper (pay-puhr) n. a substance in thin sheets used for writing, printing or drawing on or wrapping things in

park (pahrk) n. a public garden or area of ground for public use

part (pahrt) n. some but not all of something

path (path) n. a way or track made for or by people walking

party (pahrt-ee) n. a social occasion, often in somebody's home when people have fun together

patient (pay-shuhnt) n. a person receiving medical treatment

paw (paw) n. an animal's foot with claws

pay (pay) v. to give money to somebody for goods and services

peace (pees) n. a situation or a period of time in which there is no war or violence in a country

passage (pas-ij) n. a narrow way through something; corridor

past (past) gone by in time; of the time before the present

paste (payst) n. a soft wet mixture, usually made of powder and a liquid

pearl (purl) n. a small hard shiny white jewel that grows inside an oyster

pat (pat) v. to touch somebody or something gently several times with your open hand especially to show affection

pebble (peb-uh l) n. a small stone made smooth and round by water

pedal (ped-l) n. a flat bar that drives or controls a machine (e.g. a bicycle) when pressed down by the foot (see bicycle)

peek (peek) v. to take a quick look at something secretly

pen (pen) n. an instrument for writing with ink

pencil (pen-sil) n. a narrow piece of wood, containing a black or coloured substance, used for writing or drawing

penny (pen-ee) n. a small British coin and unit of money

peppermint (pep-uhr-muh nt) n. 1 a type of mint grown for its strong tasting oil
2 a sweet which is flavoured with peppermint

perfect (puhr-fikt) having everything necessary; complete and without faults

perhaps (per-haps) possibly; it may be that

person (puhr-suhn) n. a human being

pet (pet) n. an animal, e.g. a cat or dog, that you keep at home as a companion

petal (pet-l) n. the delicate coloured part of a flower

petrol (pe-truhl) n. liquid obtained from petroleum, used as fuel in car engines

photograph (foht-uh-graf) n. a picture made by using a camera that has film sensitive to light inside it

piano (pee-an-oh) n. a large musical instrument in which metal strings are struck by hammers operated by pressing black and white keys

picnic (pik-nik) n. an informal meal eaten outdoors

pie (pie) n. meat or fruit covered with pastry and baked in a dish

piece (pees) n. an amount of something that has been cut or separated from the rest

pile (pile) n. a number of things lying one upon another

pillow (pil-oh) n. a soft cushion used for supporting the head in bed

place (plays) n. position, point or area

play (play) v. 1 to take part in a game or sport
2 a story with actors performing

playground (play-ground) n. an outdoor area where children can play especially at a school

please (pleez) used as a polite way of asking for something or telling somebody to do something

pocket (pahk-uht) n. a small bag sewn into a piece of clothing so that you can carry things in it

pod (pahd) n. a long thin case filled with seeds that develops from the flowers of some plants, especially peas and beans

poem (poh-uhm) n. a piece of writing arranged in lines usually with a regular rhythm and often with a pattern of rhymes

police (puh-lees) n. someone whose job is to keep public order, prevent and solve crime

polish (pol-ish) v. to make something smooth and shiny by rubbing it

polite (puh-lite) having or showing good manners

pollen (pol-uhn) n. fine, yellow powder formed on flowers that fertilizes other flowers

poncho (pon-choh) n. a piece of cloth with a hole for the head, worn as a cloak

pond (pond) n. a small area of water

porridge (por-i j) n. soft food made by heating crushed oats in water or milk

postman (pohst-muhn) n. a person whose job is to collect and deliver letters

pour (pohr) v. to cause a liquid to flow in a continuous stream 2 (of rain) fall heavily

powder (pou-der) n. a dry mass of fine particles

power (pou-er) n. the ability to control people or things

prank (prangk) n. a trick that is played on somebody as a joke

precious (presh-uh-s) of great value

prepare (pri-pair) v. to get or make something or somebody ready to be used to do something

present (prez-uhnt) n. a thing that you give to somebody as a gift

pretend (pri-tend) v. to behave in a way that is intended to make people believe that something is true when in reality it is not

price (prahys) n. an amount of money that you have to pay for something

prince (prins) n. a male member of a royal family, especially the son of a king or queen

princess (prin-sis) n. the female member of a royal family especially the daughter of a king or queen

print (print) v. to produce letters or pictures on paper using a machine that puts ink on the surface

prison (priz-uhn) n. a building in which criminals are kept as a punishment

prize (prahyz) n. an award given for winning a competition

problem (prob-luhm) n. a thing that is difficult to deal with or understand

promise (prom-is) n. telling somebody that you will definitely do or not do something

proud (proud) having a feeling of satisfaction from doing something well or owning something

provide (pruh-vahyd) v. to give something to someone or make it available for them to use

pudding (pood-ing) n. a sweet dish eaten at the end of a meal

puddle (puhd-l) n. a small pool of water

pull (pool) v. to hold something firmly and use force in order to move it towards yourself

punch (puhnch) v. to hit somebody or something hard with your fist

pupil (pyoo-puhl) n. a person being taught, especially a child in a school

puppet (puhp-it) n. a doll that can be made to move by pulling strings attached to parts of its body or by putting your hand inside it

purse (purs) n. a small bag for carrying things especially used by women

push (poo-sh) v. to use force on something in order to move it forward, away or to a different position

puzzle (puhz-uhl) n. a game that you have to think about carefully in order to answer it or do it

pyjamas (puh-jah-muhz) n. a loose jacket and trousers worn in bed

Qq

quack (kwak) n. the sound that a duck makes

quake (kweyk) v. to shake or tremble

quality (kwol-i-tee) n. how good or bad something is

quantity (kwon-ti-tee) n. an amount or number of something

quarrel (kwawr-uhl) n. an angry argument

quarter (kwawr-ter) n. one of four equal parts of something; $\frac{1}{4}$

queasy (kwee-zee) feeling sick; wanting to vomit

queen (kween) n. the female ruler of an independent state that has a royal family

query (kweer-ee) n. a question

quick (kwik) done with speed; taking or lasting a short time

quiet (kwahy-it) making little noise

quilt (kwilt) n. a decorative padded cover for a bed

quit (kwit) v. 1 to leave your job or school
2 to stop doing something

quite (kwahyt) to some degree; fairly

quiz (kwiz) n. a game in which people are asked questions to test their knowledge

Rr

rabbit (rab-it) n. a small animal with long ears that lives in a hole in the ground

race (reys) n. a competition of speed, e.g. in running

rack (rack) n. a framework usually of metal or wooden bars, for holding things or hanging things on

racket (rak-it) n. a piece of sports equipment used for hitting the ball in tennis and squash

radio (rey-dee-oh) n. a machine for listening to radio broadcasts by a process of sending and receiving messages through the air using electromagnetic waves

raft (rahft) n. 1 a flat floating structure of logs fastened together, used as a boat 2 an inflatable rubber craft with a flat bottom

rag (rag) n. a piece of old torn cloth

railway (reyl-wey) n. the track on which trains run

rain (reyn) n. water that falls in drops from the clouds

rainbow (reyn-boh) n. a curve of many colours seen in the sky when the sun shines through rain

raincoat (reyn-koht) n. a light waterproof coat

rainfall (reyn-fawl) n. the amount of rain that falls in a certain area during a particular time

rake (reyk) n. a garden tool with a long handle and a row of metal points at the end

ranch (ranch) n. a large farm especially in the US, where cattle are bred

rank (rangk) n. the position somebody has in an organization and society or in the army and navy

rapid (rap-id) something done or happening very quickly

rare (rair) not common

razor

razor (rey-zer) n. an instrument used for shaving

reach (reech) v. to arrive at a place; achieve an aim

read (reed) v. to look at and understand something written or printed

ready (red-ee) 1 prepared and fit for action or use
2 easily available

real (ree-uhl) something true or actual

reap (reep) v. 1 to obtain something good especially as a result of hard work
2 to cut and collect a crop especially corn

receive (ree-seev) v. to get or accept something sent or given

recipe (res-uh-pee) n. a set of instructions for preparing a food dish

recite (ri-sahyt) v. to say a poem aloud from memory

R
RECITE

RECOLLECT

recollect (ree-kuh-lekt) v. to remember something

record (ri-kawrd) n. a written account of facts and events

recreation (ree-kree-ey-shuh-n) n. play or amusement or a way of spending your free time

rectangle (rek-tang-guhl) n. a flat four-sided shape with four angles of 90°c

recycle (ree-sahy-kuhl) v. to treat something already used so that it can be used again

reed (reed) n. a tall plant like grass that grows near water

reduce (ri-dyoos) v. to make something less or smaller in size, price

referee (ref-uh-ree) n. an official who controls the game in some sports

refrigerate (ri-frij-uh-reyt) v. to make food and drink cold in order to keep it fresh or preserve it

refuse (ri-fyooz) v. to not give, accept or do something

region (ree-juhn) n. 1 a large area of land
2 division of a country

regret (ri-gret) v. to be sorry or sad about something

regular (reg-yuh-ler) something happening or coming repeatedly at times or places that are the same distance apart

reel (reel) n. a cylinder on which thread, wire, film is wound

reindeer (reyn-deer) n. a large deer with antlers, living in cold northern regions

rejoice (ri-jois) v. to express great happiness about something

relax (ri-laks) v. to rest while you are doing something enjoyable especially after work

religion (ri-lij-uhn) n. the belief in and worship of God or gods

relish (rel-ish) n. great enjoyment

remark (ri-mahrk) v. to say or write a comment about something or somebody

remember (ri-mem-ber) v. to have or keep an image in your memory; bring back to your mind something that you knew

remind (ri-mahynd) v. to help somebody to remember something important that they must do

remove (ri-moov) v. to take something or somebody away or off

rent (rent) n. the money paid regularly for the use of a house or building

repair (ri-pair) v. to mend something broken, damaged or torn

repeat (ri-peet) v. to say or write something again or more than once

reply (ri-plahy) v. to give something as an answer to something or somebody

request (ri-kwest) n. an act of politely asking for something

require (ri-kwahy-uhr) v. to need something or depend on something

rescue (res-kyoo) v. to save something or somebody from a dangerous or harmful situation

rest (rest) 1 a period of relaxing or sleeping
2 the remaining part of something

restaurant (res-ter-uhnt) n. a place where meals can be bought and eaten

return (ri-turn) v. to come or go back

reward (ri-ward) n. something given in return for work or services or for bringing back stolen property

rhyme (rahym) v. words ending with the same sound

rhythm (rith-uhm) n. a regular pattern of beats or movements

rib (rib) n. the curved bones that go from the backbone to the chest (see skeleton)

ribbon (rib-uhn) n. narrow strips of material used to tie things or for decoration

rice (rahys) n. white or brown grain that is cooked and eaten

rich (rich) having a lot of money or property

rickshaw (rik-shaw) n. a small light vehicle with two wheels that is pulled by somebody walking or riding a bicycle

riddle (rid-l) n. a difficult or amusing question

ride (rahyd) v. to sit on a horse or bicycle and control it as it moves

ridicule (rid-i-kyool) n. unkind comments that make fun of somebody

rifle (rahy-fuhl) n. a gun with a long barrel, fired from the shoulder (see weapon)

right (rahyt) 1 morally good or acceptable
2 exactly; directly

ring (ring) n. a circular metal band worn on a finger

rinse (rins) v. to wash something in clean water

ripe (rahyp) something fully grown and ready to be eaten

rise (rahyz) v. to come or go upwards

river (riv-er) n. a large natural stream of water flowing to the sea

road (rohd) n. a hard surface built for vehicles to travel on

roam (rohm) v. to walk or travel about with no clear purpose

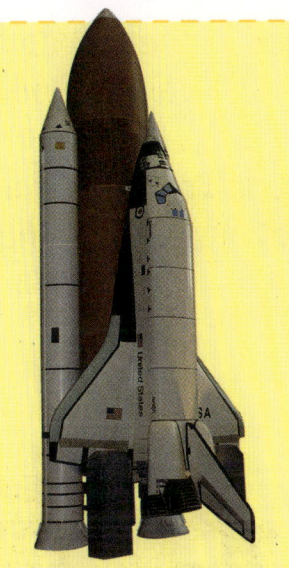

rocket (rok-it) n. a tube-shaped device filled with fast-burning fuel that is used to launch a missile or spacecraft

rod (rod) n. a long thin straight piece of wood or metal

robot (roh-buht) n. a machine that can do certain human tasks automatically

rock (rok) 1 a large stone 2 to move gently backwards and forwards or from side to side

rodent (rohd-nt) n. a small animal, e.g. a rat, with strong sharp front teeth.

rogue (rohg) n. a person who behaves badly but in a harmless way

roll (rohl) v. to make a round object move along by turning over and over

R

ROLL

63

R

roof (roof) n. the top covering of a building or a car (see house)

room (room) n. part of a building with its own walls, ceiling and door

root (root) n. part of a plant that is in the soil and takes in water and food from the soil

rope (rohp) n. a very thick strong string

rose (rohz) n. a flower with a sweet smell

rotate (roh-teyt) v. to cause something to move or turn around a central point

rough (ruhf) 1 a surface not level or smooth 2 not exact; not in detail

round (round) shaped like a circle or a ball; curved

route (root) n. the way from one place to another

routine (roo-teen) n. a regular way of doing things

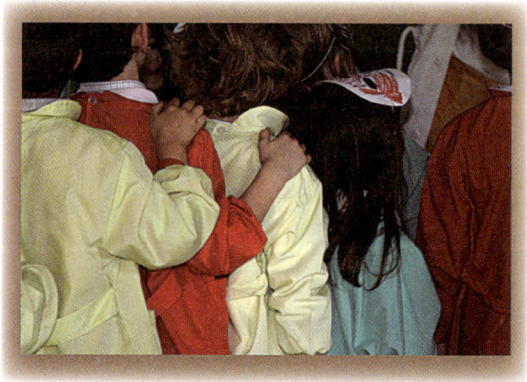

row (roh) n. 1 a line of people or things
2 a journey in a rowing boat

royal (roi-uhl) of or belonging to a king or queen

rubber (ruhb-er) n. 1 a strong elastic substance used for making tyres
2 a piece of rubber for removing pencil marks from paper

rug (ruhg) n. a thick piece of material, like a small carpet, for covering part of a floor

run (ruhn) v. to move using your legs, going faster than when you walk

rugby (ruhg-bee) n. a kind of football played with an oval ball that may be kicked or carried

rush (ruhsh) v. to move or do something with great speed, often too fast

ruin (roo-in) v. to destroy or spoil something

rule (rool) n. a statement of what may, must or must not be done

rusk (ruhsk) n. hard crisp biscuit for babies to eat.

rumour (roo-muh) n. a piece of information spread by being talked about but not certainly true

rust (ruhst) n. a reddish-brown substance formed on metal by the action of water and air

R

RUST

Ss

SACK

sack (sak) n. a large bag of strong material for carrying coal, potatoes and many other things

sad (sad) unhappy

saddle (sad-l) n. a leather seat for a rider on a horse or bicycle

safe (seyf) protected from danger and harm

sail (seyl) v. to travel on water in a ship or yacht

salt (sawlt) n. white substance obtained from mines and sea water, used to flavour food

same (seym) exactly like something

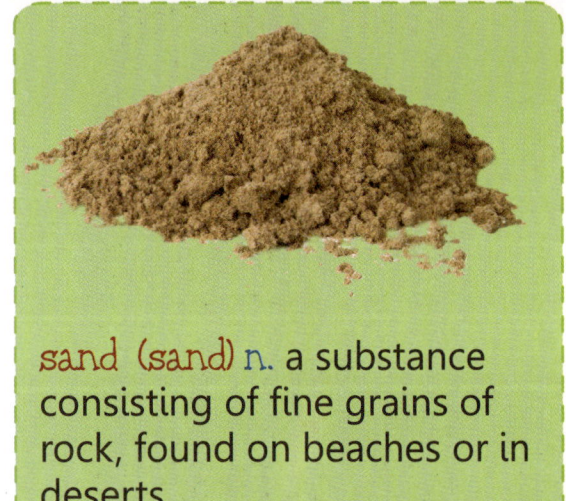

sand (sand) n. a substance consisting of fine grains of rock, found on beaches or in deserts

save (seyv) v. 1 to keep somebody or something safe from harm or loss
2 keep something especially money for future use

saw (saw) n. a tool which has a long blade with sharp teeth, for cutting wood and metal

say (sey) v. to speak or tell something to somebody, using words

scalp (skalp) n. the skin and hair on top of the head

scare (skair) v. to frighten somebody

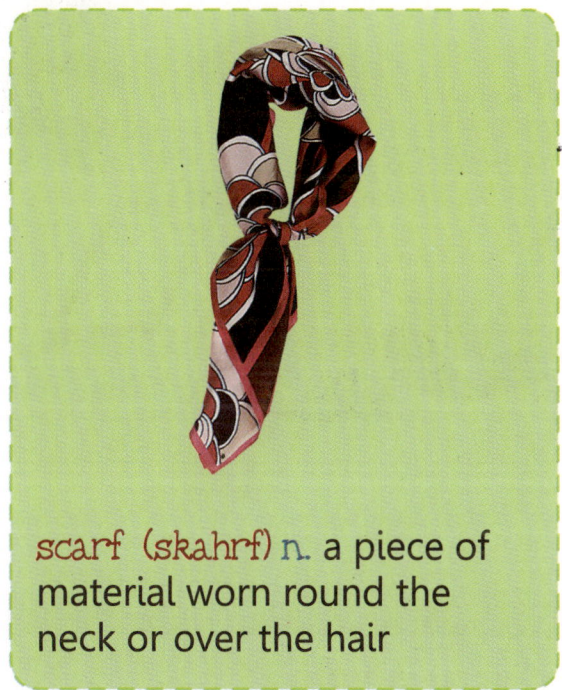

scarf (skahrf) n. a piece of material worn round the neck or over the hair

scatter (skat-er) v. to throw or drop things in different directions

school (skool) n. a place where children go to be educated or where people go to learn a particular skill

science (sahy-uh ns) n. the knowledge about the structure and behaviour of the natural and physical world, based on facts that you can prove, e.g. by experiments

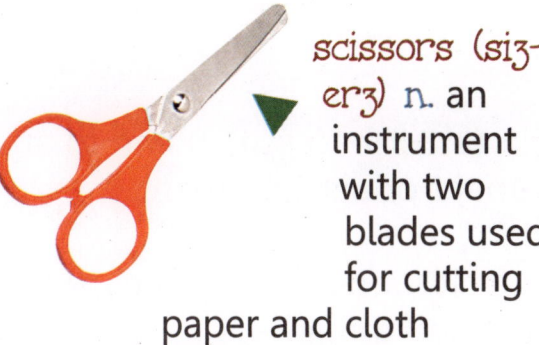

scissors (siz-erz) n. an instrument with two blades used for cutting paper and cloth

scold (skohld) v. to speak angrily to somebody especially a child

scooter (skoo-ter) n. a light motorcycle with a small engine and a cover to protect the rider's legs

score (skohr) v. to win points or goals in a, game

scout (skout) n. an organization originally for boys, that trains young people in practical skills

scream (skreem) v. to give a long sharp cry of fear, pain or anger

scribble (skrib-uhl) v. to write something quickly and carelessly

sea (see) n. salt water that covers most of the earth's surface

seal (seel) n. a sea animal that eats fish and lives around coasts
2 to close an envelope by sticking the edges of the opening together

search (surch) v. to look carefully for somebody or something; examine a particular place when looking for somebody or something

season (see-zuhn) n. any of the four main periods of the year

seat (seet) n. a place where you can sit

secret (see-krit) to be kept from the knowledge or view of others

seed (seed) n. the small hard part of a plant from which a new plant can grow

seem (seem) v. to give the appearance of being or doing something

see-saw (see-saw) n. a long plank supported in the middle, with a person sitting at each end, rising and falling in turn

sell (sel) v. to give something to somebody in exchange for money

sentence (sen-tns) n. a group of words that express a statement or question

separate (sep-uh-reyt) v. to move apart; divide into different parts or groups

set (set) n. a group of similar things of the same kind that belong together

settle (set-l) v. to put an end to an argument or disagreement

sew (soh) v. to make stitches with a needle and thread

shake (sheyk) v. 1 to cause somebody or something to move quickly from side to side or up and down
2 to make short quick movements that you cannot control, e.g. because you are afraid

share (shair) n. to divide something between two or more people

sharp (shahrp) having a fine cutting edge or point

shave (sheyv) v. to cut hair off the face with a razor

shed (shed) n. a small building, usually of wood, used for storing things

shell (shel) n. a hard outer covering of eggs, nuts and some animals, e.g. snails

shelter (shel-ter) n. 1 a place to live or stay
2 protection from rain, danger or attack

shepherd (shep-erd) n. a person who takes care of sheep

shine (shahyn) v. to give out or reflect light
2 to polish something

ship (ship) n. a large boat that carries people or goods by sea

shirt (shurt) n. a piece of clothing for the upper part of the body

shoe (shoo) n. someting worn on your feet

shoot (shoot) v. 1 to aim and fire with a gun or other weapon
2 to make a film or photograph of something

shop (shop) n. a building where goods are sold

short (shawrt) not long

shoulder (shohl-der) n. either of the two parts of the body between the top of each arm and the neck

show (shoh) v. to let somebody see something

S

SHUT

shut (shuht) v. 1 to become closed
2 to stop being open for business

◀ **sick** (sik) ill

sight (sahyt) n. the ability to see

silent (sahy-luhnt) making little or no sound

silly (sil-ee) showing a lack of thought or good sense; foolish

simple (sim-puhl) easily understood; not difficult

◀ **sing** (sing) v. to make musical sounds with your voice in the form of a song or tune

sink (singk) v. to go down below the surface or towards the bottom of a liquid or something soft

▲ **size** (sahyz) n. how large a person or thing is

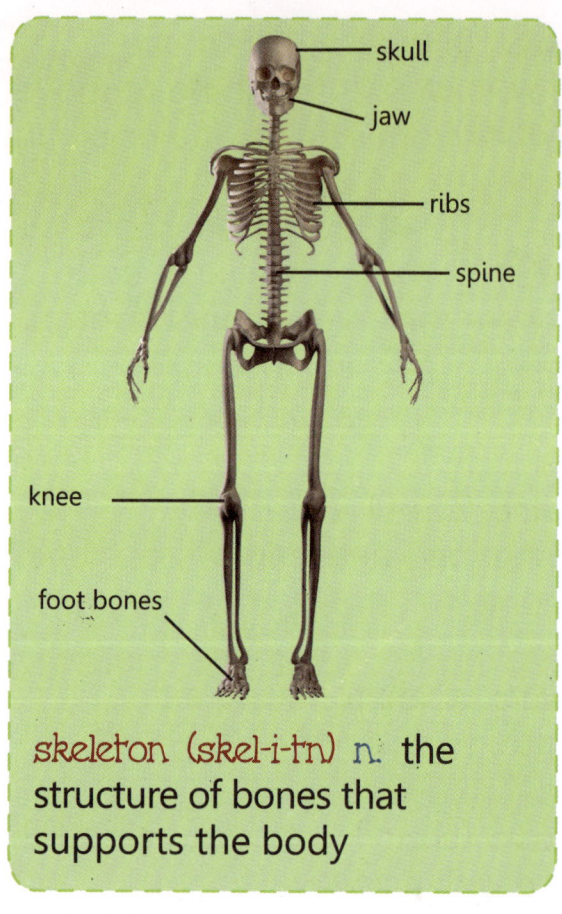

skeleton (skel-i-tn) n. the structure of bones that supports the body

sketch (skech) n. a simple drawing that is done quickly and without detail

ski (skee) v. to move over snow on skis especially as a sport

skill (skil) n. the ability to do something well

skin (skin) n. a layer of tissue that covers the body

skip (skip) v. to move forward lightly and quickly making a little jump with each step ▶

skirt (skurt) n. a piece of women's clothing that hangs from the waist

skull (skuhl) n. the bone structure that forms the head

sky (skahy) n. the space above the earth, where we see clouds, the sun, moon and stars

sleep (sleep) v. to rest with your eyes closed and your mind and body not active

sleeve (sleev) n. part of a piece of clothing that covers the arm

slide (slahyd) v. to move smoothly over a smooth or wet surface

sling (sling) n. a band of material looped round an object, e.g. a broken arm, to support or lift it

slow (sloh) taking a long time; not fast

sly (slahy) acting or done in a secret and dishonest way

small (smawl) not large in size, little in size

smart (smahrt) 1 clean and neat; well dressed 2 intelligent

smell (smel) n. the quality of something that people and animals sense through their noses

smile (smahyl) n. an expression of the face with the corners of the mouth turned up, showing amusement and happiness

smooth (smooth) completely flat and even, without any lumps or holes

sneeze (sneez) v. to have air come noisily and uncontrollably out through your nose and mouth, e.g. because you have a cold

snow (snoh) n. frozen water falling from the sky in soft, white flakes

soak (sohk) v. to put something in liquid for a time so that it becomes completely wet

soap (sohp) n. a substance used with water for washing your body

sob (sob) v. to cry noisily, taking sudden sharp breaths

sock (sok) n. a piece of clothing worn over the foot and ankle especially inside a shoe

soft (sawft) 1 not hard or stiff 2 smooth and pleasant to touch

soil (soil) n. the upper layer of earth in which plants grow

some (suhm) an unspecified number or amount

song (sawng) n. a short piece of music with words that you sing

soon (soon) a short time from now; a short time after something else has happened

sorry (sor-ee) feeling sad and ashamed about something that has been done

sound (sound) n. something that you can hear

soup (soop) n. liquid food made by cooking meat and vegetables together in water

sow (soh) v. plant or spread seeds in or on the ground

speak (speek) v. to talk to somebody about something; to use your voice to say something

special (spesh-uhl) of a particular kind; not common

spell (spel) v. to say or write the letters of a word in the correct order

spend (spend) v. to use money to pay for goods and services

spider (spahy-der) n. a small creature with eight legs

spin (spin) v. to turn round and round quickly

spinach (spin-ich) n. a plant with large green leaves, cooked and eaten as a vegetable

split (split) v. to divide something into separate parts

spoil (spoil) v. to ruin something

spoon (spoon) n. a utensil with a shallow bowl on a handle, used for putting food, e.g. soup, into the mouth

sport (spohrt) n. an activity done for pleasure or exercise usually according to rules

spot (spot) n. a small dirty mark on something

spring (spring) v. 1 to jump or move suddenly 2 the season of the year between winter and summer, when plants begin to grow

square (skwair) having four straight equal sides and four angles of 90

squash (skwosh) v. to press something so that it becomes soft, damaged or flat

squeeze (skweez) v. to press something firmly especially with your fingers

squirrel (skwur-uhl) n. a small bushy-tailed animal with red or grey fur

S

SQUIRREL

stair (stair) n. a set of steps built between two floors inside a building

stamp (stamp) a small piece of printed paper stuck on envelopes or parcels to show that postage has been paid
2 to put your foot down with force on the ground

stand (stand) v. to be on your feet; be upright

star (stahr) n. a large ball of burning gas seen as a point of light in the sky at night

start (stahrt) v. to begin doing something

stay (stey) v. to be or remain in the same place or condition

steal (steel) v. to take something which is not yours

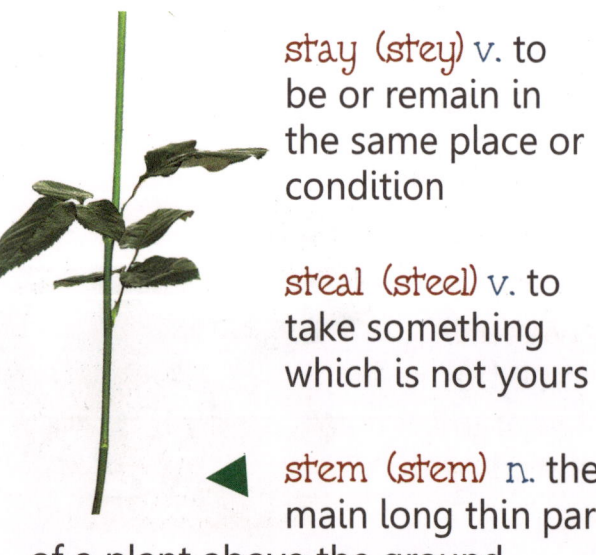

stem (stem) n. the main long thin part of a plant above the ground

step (step) v. to lift your foot and move it in a particular direction or put it on or in something

stick (stik) 1 to be fixed to something else, especially with glue
2 a small thin piece of wood that has fallen from a tree

still (stil) not moving; calm and quiet

sting (sting) n. a sharp, often poisonous organ of some insects, e.g. bees

stink (stingk) v. to have a strong unpleasant smell

stir (stur) v. to mix a liquid by moving a spoon round and round in it

stitch (stich) n. the single passing of a needle and thread through cloth to join or decorate something, or through skin to close a wound

S

stone (stohn) n. a solid mineral substance found in the ground used for building

stool (stool) n. a small seat without a back

stop (stop) v. to no longer move or function

storm (stawrm) n. a period of very strong winds, rain, thunder and lightning

straight (streyt) not bent or curved

straw (straw) n. a thin tube of plastic that you suck a drink through

stream (streem) n. a small narrow river

street (street) n. a road with houses and buildings on one or both sides

strength (strengkth) n. the quality or degree of being strong

stretch (strech) v. to make something wider, longer or looser by pulling it

string (string) n. a fine cord for tying things

stroke (strohk) v. to move your hand gently over a surface

strong (strawng) having great power

sudden (suhd-n) happening unexpectedly and quickly

sugar (shoog-er) n. a sweet substance obtained from various plants

S

SUMMER

summer (suhm-er) n. the warmest season of the year

swift (swift) being quick and prompt

sun (suhn) n. the bright yellow star round which the earth moves and which gives it heat and light

super (su-pur) adj. excellent

surprise (ser-prahyz) n. something sudden or unexpected

swallow (swol-oh) v. to cause food to go down your throat

swim (swim) v. to move through water using the arms and legs

sweat (swet) n. liquid which comes through the skin when you are hot or nervous

sweep (sweep) v. clear dust, dirt, etc. using a brush, broom,

sword (sawrd) n. a weapon with a long steel blade fixed in a handle

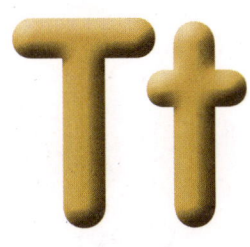

T

table (tey-buhl) n. a piece of furniture with a flat top on legs

tadpole (tad-pohl) n. a small creature that grows into a frog or toad

tail (teyl) n. the long movable part at the end of the body of an animal or bird

tailor (tey-ler) n. a person who makes clothes

tale (teyl) n. a story

talent (tal-uhnt) n. the natural ability to do something well

talk (tawk) v. to say things; speak to give information

tall (tawl) higher than average height; not short

tap (tap) n. a device for controlling the flow of liquid or gas from a pipe or container

target (tahr-git) n. the result that you try to achieve

task (tahsk) n. a piece of work that has to be done

taste (teyst) n. a quality that different foods and drinks have that allows you to recognize them when you put them in your mouth

taxi (tak-see) n. a car with a driver which may be hired

tea (tee) n. hot drink made by pouring boiling water onto tea leaves

teach (teech) v. to give lessons to somebody

team (teem) n. a group of people playing on the same side in a game

tear (teer) 1 to damage something by pulling it apart or into pieces or by cutting it on something sharp
2 a drop of liquid that comes from your eye when you cry

tease (teez) v. to laugh at somebody and make fun of them playfully or unkindly

teddy bear (ted-ee bair) n. a soft furry toy bear

telephone (tel-uh-fohn) n. a machine used in a system for talking to somebody over long distances using wires or radio

telescope (tel-uh-skohp) n. a long tube-shaped instrument with lenses, for making distant objects appear nearer and larger

television (tel-uh-vizh-uh n) n. a machine which has a screen on which you can watch moving pictures and sounds

tell (tel) v. to make something known to somebody in words

tennis (ten-is) n. a game for two or four players who hit a ball across a net with a racket

tent (tent) n. a shelter made of cloth that is supported by poles and ropes and is used for camping

terror (ter-er) n. a feeling of extreme fear

test (test) n. an examination of a person's knowledge or ability

thank (thangk) v. to tell somebody that you are grateful for something

theft (theft) n. a crime of stealing something from a person or place

their (thair) of or belonging to them

then (then) at that time

thick (thik) not thin

thief (theef) n. a person who steals something from another person or place

thin (thin) not fat

think (thingk) v. to use your mind to form opinions and make decisions

thirst (thurst) n. a feeling of needing or wanting a drink

thorn (thawrn) n. a sharp pointed part on the stem of some plants, e.g. roses

thorough (thur-oh) done completely and carefully

thrill (thril) n. a strong feeling of excitement or pleasure

throne (throhn) n. a special chair used by a king or queen in official ceremonies

throw (throh) v. to send something through the air with some force, especially by moving the arm

thug (thuhg) n. a violent and dangerous person

thumb (thuhm) n. a short thick finger set apart from the other four

thunder (thuhn-der) n. a loud noise that follows a flash of lightning

tiara (tee-ar-uh) n. a piece of jewellery like a small crown, worn by a woman

ticket (tik-it) n. a printed piece of card or paper that gives you the right to travel on a bus or enter a cinema

tickle (tik-uh l) v. to touch part of somebody's body

tidy (tahy-dee) neat and orderly

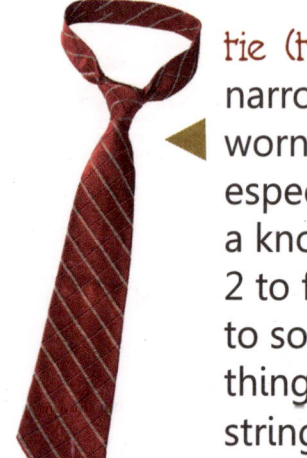

tie (tahy) 1 a long narrow strip of material worn round the neck especially by men with a knot at the front 2 to fasten something to something or hold things together using a string or rope

tight (tahyt) held or fixed in position firmly; not loose

till (til) n. a drawer or box for money in a shop or bank

time (tahym) n. what is measured in minutes, hours, days

tin (tin) n. a soft silver-white metal

tinkle (tingk-huhl) v. to make a series of light high ringing sounds

tinsel (tin-suhl) n. a strip or thread of shiny material used as a Christmas decoration

tiny (tahy-nee) extremely small

tiptoe (tip-toh) v. to walk quietly

tissue (tish-oo) n. a piece of soft paper used as a handkerchief

title (tahyt-l) n. the name of a book, play or picture

today (tuh-dey) n. on this day

toffee (taw-fee) n. a hard sticky sweet made by heating sugar with butter

tomorrow (tuh-mawr-oh) n. the day after today

tonight (tuh-nahyt) n. during the evening or night of today

tool (tool) n. an instrument that you hold in your hand and use for working on something

tooth (tooth) n. any of the hard white objects in the mouth, used for biting and chewing food

top (top) n. the highest part or point of something

torch (tawrch) n. a small electric light held in the hand

toss (taws) v. to throw something lightly or carelessly

total (toht-l) n. the complete number or amount

touch (tuhch) v. to put your hands or fingers onto somebody or something

tour (toor) n. a journey made for pleasure during which several places are visited

towel (tou-uhl) n. a piece of fabric or paper for wiping or drying

town (tou-n) n. a place with many buildings and houses, larger than a village

toy (toi) n. a thing for children to play with

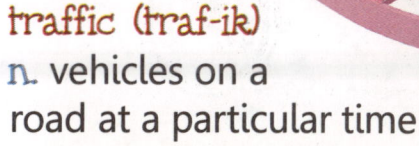

traffic (traf-ik) n. vehicles on a road at a particular time

train (treyn) n. a line of carriages or trucks joined together and pulled along by a railway engine

T

TRAIN

81

T
TRAVEL

travel (trav-uhl) v. to go from one place to another, especially over a long distance

tree (tree) n. a tall plant with a wooden trunk, branches and leaves

triangle (trahy-ang-guh l) n. a flat shape with three straight sides and three angles

tricycle (trahy-si-kuhl) n. a vehicle like a bicycle, but with one wheel at the front and two behind

trophy (troh-fee) n. a prize given for winning a competition

trouble (truhb-uhl) n. a problem, worry or difficulty

trousers (trou-zer) n. a piece of clothing that covers the body from the waist down and is divided into two to cover each leg separately

true (troo) connected with facts rather than things that have been invented or guessed

trunk (truhngk) n. the thick main stem of a tree

try (trahy) v. to make an attempt to do or get something

tub (tub) n. an open container, used for washing clothes in

tulip (too-lip) n. a large brightly coloured spring flower, shaped like a cup, on a tall stem

tune (tyoon) n. a series of musical notes that are sung or played in a particular order

tunnel (tuhn-l) n. an underground passage, e.g. for a road or railway

turn (turn) v. to move around

tutor (tutor) n. a private teacher especially of one pupil

twin (twin) n. either of two children born to the same mother at one time

twist (twist) v. to bend or turn into a particular shape

twitter (twitter) v. to make light chirping sounds like a bird

typewriter (tahyp-rahy-tur) n. a machine that prints letters on paper by means of keys that are pressed with the fingers

tyre (tahyuhr) n. a thick rubber ring that fits around the edge of a wheel of a bicycle or car *(see bicycle)*

Uu

UFO (yoo-ef-oh) n. an Unidentified Flying Object, especially a spacecraft believed to have come from another planet

ugly (uhg-lee) unpleasant to look at

umbrella (uhm-brel-uh) n. a folding frame covered with cloth used as a protection from the rain or sun

unable (uhn-ey-buhl) not having the skill, strength, knowledge to do something

unbutton (uhn-buht-n) v. to undo the buttons on a piece of clothing

uncle (uhng-kuhl) n. the brother of your father or mother; husband of your aunt

under (uhn-der) below something

understand (uhn-der-stand) v. to know or realize the meaning of words, a language and what somebody says

underwater (uhn-der-waw-ter) found, used or happening below the surface of water

underwear (uhn-der-wair) n. clothing worn next to the skin and under other clothes

undress (uhn-dres) v. to take off your clothes; remove somebody else's clothes

uneven (uhn-ee-vuhn) not level or smooth

unfair (uhn-fair) not right or just

unhappy (uhn-hap-ee) not happy; sad

unicorn (yoo-ni-kawrn) n. (in stories) a white horse with a long straight horn on its forehead

uniform (yoo-nuh-fawrm) n. a special set of clothes worn by all members of an organization or group, e.g. the army or school children

universe (yoo-nuh-vurs) n. everything that exists in space, including all the stars and planets

unkind (uhn-kahynd) unpleasant or unfriendly; slightly cruel

unlike (uhn-lahyk) different from a particular person or thing

unlucky (uhn-luhk-ee) having or bringing bad luck

untidy (uhn-tahy-dee) not neat or ordered

until (uhn-til) up to the point in time or the event mentioned

up (uhp) towards or in a higher position

upset (uhp-set) unhappy or disappointed because of something unpleasant that has happened

upstairs (uhp-stairz) to or on a higher floor

upward (uhp-werd) pointing towards or facing a higher place

urgent (ur-juh nt) needing to be dealt with immediately

us (uhs) me and another or others; me and you

use (yooz) v. to do something with a machine, a method or an object for a particular purpose

Vv

VALLEY

valley (val-ee) n. a low land between hills or mountains, often with a river

value (val-yoo) n. what a thing is worth

van (van) n. a covered vehicle with no side windows used for carrying goods

vanilla (vuh-nil-uh) n. a flavouring that comes from a plant and is used in sweet foods, e.g. ice cream

vase (vahs) n. a container made of glass or clay used especially for holding cut flowers

vast (vah-st) extremely large

vegetable (vej-tuh-buh l) n. a plant, e.g. potato, bean or onion, eaten as food

vehicle (vee-i-kuh l) n. something such as a car, bus or lorry that carries people or goods from place to place

verb (vurb) n. a word or phrase that expresses an action

very (ver-ee) to a great degree; extremely

victory (vik-tuh-ree) n. success in a game, an election or a war

video (video) n. a box containing a type of magnetic tape used for recording moving pictures and sound

86

view (view) n. a personal opinion about something; attitude towards something

village (vil-ij) n. a very small town situated in a country area

villain (villain) n. a criminal

vinegar (vin-i-ger) n. a bitter liquid made from malt, wine used to add flavour to food or to preserve it

◄ **violet** (vahy-uh-let) n. 1 a small plant with sweet-smelling purple or white flowers 2 bluish-purple colour

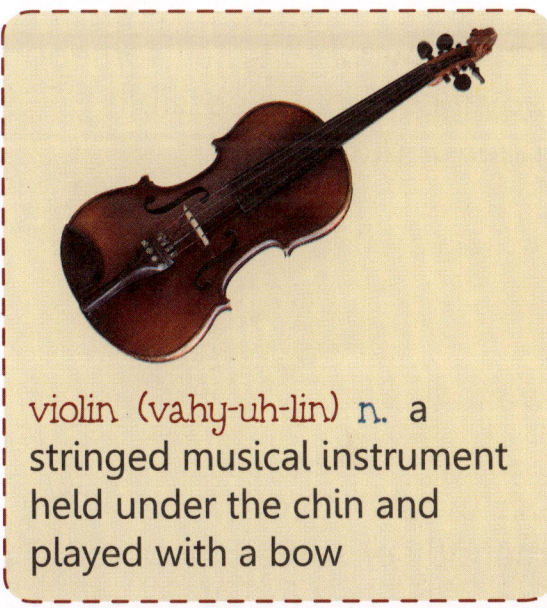

violin (vahy-uh-lin) n. a stringed musical instrument held under the chin and played with a bow

visit (viz-it) v. to go to see a person or place for a period of time

voice (vois) n. the sounds produced through the mouth by a person speaking or singing

volcano (vol-key-noh) n. a mountain with an opening through which hot melted rock and gas are forced out

a e i
o u
▲
vowel (vou-uhl) n. a letter that represents a vowel sound, e.g. a, e, i, o and u

Ww

waffle (wof-uhl) n. a small crisp pancake with a pattern of raised squares

wag (wag) v. to move from side to side

wait (weyt) v. to stay where you are or delay doing something until somebody or something comes or something happens

wake (weyk) v. to stop sleeping

walk (wawk) v. to move or go somewhere by putting one foot in front of the other on the ground, but without running

wall (wawl) n. a long upright solid structure of stone or brick that surrounds, divides or protects something

wallet (wol-it) n. a small flat case, especially for carrying paper money and credit cards

wardrobe (wawr-drohb) n. a tall cupboard for hanging clothes in

warm (wawrm) fairly hot; between cool and hot

warn (wawrn) v. to tell somebody in advance about a possible danger or difficulty

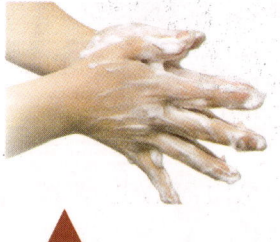

wash (wosh) v. to make somebody or something clean using water and usually soap

waste (weyst) v. to not make good or full use of somebody or something

watch (woch) 1 a small clock worn on the wrist 2 to look at somebody or something carefully for a period of time

water (wot-er) n. a clear colourless liquid that falls as rain, is found in rivers and is used for drinking

wave (weyv) v. to move your hand or arm from side to side in the air to attract attention, as a greeting

way (wey) n. 1 a method, style or manner of doing something 2 the route or road that you take in order to reach a place

weak (week) not physically strong

grenade launcher
pistol
axe
uzi
shotgun slingshot

weapon (wep-uh n) n. something, e.g. a gun, bomb or sword, used in fighting

wear (wair) v. to have something on your body, e.g. a piece of clothing or an ornament

weather (weth -er) n. the condition of sun, wind, rain or snow at a particular place and time

week (week) n. a period of seven days especially from Monday to Sunday

welcome (wel-kuh m) v. to greet somebody in a friendly way when they arrive somewhere

well (wel) 1 a deep hole in the ground from which people obtain water 2 in a good, right or satisfactory way

wet (wet) covered or soaked with liquid especially water

wheat (hweet) n. grain from which flour is made

W

WHEAT

wheel (hweel) n. one of the circular objects under a car or bicycle that turns when it moves *(see bicycle)*

while (hwahyl) during the time that something is happening

whiskers

whisker (hwis-ker) n. the long stiff hair near the mouth of a cat and many other animals

whisper (hwis-per) v. to speak very quietly to somebody so that others cannot hear what you are saying

whole (hohl) full; complete

wicked (wik-id) evil or morally bad

wide (wahyd) measuring a lot from one side to the other

win (win) v. to be the most successful in a game or competition

wind (wind) n. the air that moves quickly as a result of natural forces

window (win-doh) n. an opening in a wall or vehicle to let in light and air

wings

wing (wing) n. one of the parts of the body of a bird, insect or plane that it uses for flying

wipe (wahyp) v. to rub a surface with a cloth or your hand in order to remove dirt or liquid from it

wise (wahyz) having or showing experience, knowledge and common sense

wish (wish) v. to want something to happen or be true even though it is unlikely or impossible

witch (wich) n. a woman believed to have evil magic powers

wool (wool) n. the soft hair of sheep and some other animals

wizard (wiz-erd) n. 1 a man believed to have magic powers 2 a person who is very good at something

woman (woom-uhn) n. an adult female human being

wolf (wolf) n. a fierce wild animal of the dog family

wonder (wuhn-der) v. to feel curious about something; ask yourself about something

wood (wood) n. the hard material that the trunk and branches of a tree are made of

work (wurk) v. to do something that requires mental or physical effort, especially as part of a job

world (wurld) n. the earth, its countries and people

worm (wurm) n. a small long thin creature with no bones or legs

worry (wur-ee) v. to be anxious about somebody or something

worse (wurs) of poorer quality or lower standard; less good

would (wood) v. used as the past form of will when reporting what somebody has said or thought

wrap (rap) v. to cover something completely with something

wrestle (res-uh l) v. to fight somebody by holding them and trying to throw them to the ground

write (rahyt) v. to mark letters or numbers on a surface, especially with a pen or pencil

wrong (rawng) not true or correct; mistaken

Xx

Xmas (kris-muhs or eks-muhs) n. used as a short way of writing 'Christmas'

X-ray (eks-rey) n. a type of radiation that can pass through objects and make it possible to see inside them

xylophone (zahy-luh-fohn) n. a musical instrument with a row of wooden bars that are hit with small wooden hammers

Yy

yacht (yot) n. a large sailing boat, often with an engine and a place to sleep on board, used for pleasure trips and racing

yarn (yahrn) n. a thread that has been spun for knitting and weaving

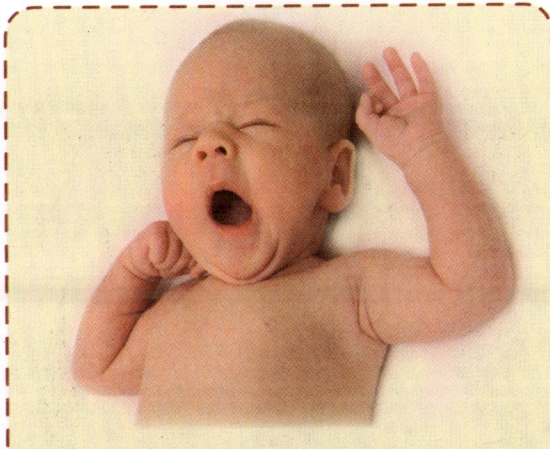

yawn (yawn) v. to open your mouth wide and breathe in deeply usually because you are tired or bored

year (yeer) n. a period of 365 days (or 366) from 1 January to 31 December

yell (yel) v. to shout loudly

yoghurt (yoh-gert) n. a thick white liquid food made by adding bacteria to milk and often flavoured with fruit

yolk (yohlk) n. the yellow part of an egg

you (yoo) a person or people being spoken to or written to

young (yuhng) having lived or existed for a short time

your (yohr) belonging to you

youth (yooth) n. the time or state of being young

yo-yo (yoh-yoh) n. a toy which is round and has a string tied to it so it can go up and down

Zz

ZEBRA

zebra (zee-bruh) n. an African wild animal like a horse with black and white stripes on its body

zero (zeer-oh) nothing

zigzag (zig-zag) n. a line that turns right and left at sharp angles

zip (zip) (also zip fastener) n. a device used for fastening clothes and bags consisting of two rows of metal or plastic teeth that you can pull together to close something or pull apart to open it

zodiac (zodiac) n. (the zodiac) an imaginary band in the sky containing the positions of the sun, moon and planets, divided into twelve equal parts

zone (zohn) n. an area or region with particular features or uses

zoo (zoo) n. a park where living animals are kept for people to look at

zoology (zoo-awl-jee) n. the scientific study of animals and their behaviour

zoom (zoom) v. to move or go somewhere very fast